NEWFOUNDLAND
& LABRADOR

ANDREW HEMPSTEAD

LABRADOR

NEWFOUNDLAND
AND LABRADOR

ATLANTIC
OCEAN

Ungava
Bay

ATLANTIC

Torngat
Mountains
National Park

Torngat Mountains

▲ Mt Caubvick
1,652m
HEBRON ★

Labrador
Sea

QUÉBEC

Kaumajet
Mountains

Kiglapait
Mountains

O C E A N

0   50 mi
0   50 km

Lake
Champdoré

Nain

Davis Inlet

Hopedale

Schefferville

Postville   Makkovik

NEWFOUNDLAND
AND LABRADOR

Rigolet

GANNET ISLANDS
ECOLOGICAL RESERVE
★

Esker

Michikamau
Lake

Lake
Melville

Churchill
Falls

North West River

Hamilton
Inlet

Cartwright

Happy Valley-Goose Bay

Mealy
Mountains

Black
Tickle

Labrador
City

Mud
Lake

Wabush

Churchill   *River*

389

Battle
Harbour

TRANSLABRADOR
HWY

Mary's Harbour

Cape
Charles

To Baie-Comeau

Red Bay

510

West
St. Modeste

L'Anse-au-Loup

QUÉBEC

Blanc Sablon   L'Anse-Amour

Forteau

L'Anse-au
-Clair

St.
Anthony

St. Barbe

Newfoundland

430

Sept-Iles

Strait of Belle Isle

Port au
Choix

Hawke's
Bay

© AVALON TRAVEL

Contents

**Discover
Newfoundland & Labrador . . 6**
The Best of Newfoundland &
Labrador 8

**St. John's and the Avalon
Peninsula** **10**
Sights 16
Recreation 24
Entertainment and Events 25
Shopping 27
Food 28
Accommodations and Camping 30
Information and Services 33
Getting There and Around 33
Avalon Peninsula 35

**Central and Western
Newfoundland** **42**
Burin Peninsula and Vicinity 46
Bonavista Peninsula 49
Clarenville to Deer Lake 53
Deer Lake to Port-aux-Basques 59
Gros Morne National Park 66

Labrador **83**
Labrador Straits 88
Central Labrador 94
North Coast 98

Background **102**
The Landscape 103
Plants and Animals 105
History 110
Government and Economy 116
People and Culture 118

Essentials **121**
Transportation 122
Recreation 124
Accommodations 127
Travel Tips 130
Health and Safety 131
Information and Services 133

Resources **135**
Suggested Reading 135
Internet Resources 137

Index **139**

List of Maps **143**

DISCOVER

Newfoundland & Labrador

Majestic icebergs wander into fjords and coves on the northern coastlines of Newfoundland. All along the seacoasts, photogenic lighthouses perch atop precipitous cliffs overlooking the surf. Sightseers line up for boat tours led by knowledgeable skippers and academically trained guides, whose vessels nose among whales, seals, and ice.

Labrador, called "the land of stone and rocks" by explorer Jacques Cartier, offers a different type of adventure. Resembling an irregular wedge pointing toward the North Pole, Labrador is bordered on the east by 8,000 kilometers of coastline on the Labrador Sea, and on the west and south by the remote outskirts of Québec. Anglers come from all over for some of the world's best sportfishing, while serious explorers venture out into the wilderness of the Torgnat Mountains.

Newfoundland and Labrador are full of history, coastal beauty, and rugged excursions. But some of your most treasured memories will be of the people. The seafaring life has given them what so much of the modern world has let slip through its fingers. Enjoy these refuges, where the friendly residents will make you feel welcome.

Clockwise from top left: Western Brook Pond; Commissariat House in St. John's; fox; Lobster Cove Head Lighthouse; moose; loon.

The Best of Newfoundland & Labrador

Day 1

Start in **St. John's,** Newfoundland's provincial capital, then head to **The Rooms** to learn about local history and **Signal Hill National Historic Site** for the views. Spend late afternoon exploring the charming village of **Quidi Vidi,** where you have reservations at **Mallard Cottage** for dinner. Still feeling energetic? The downtown bars of **George Street** come alive after dark.

Day 2

Today is spent exploring the **Avalon Peninsula.** After a whale-watching tour of **Witless Bay Ecological Reserve,** continue south to **Ferryland.** Here, **Lighthouse Picnics** serves up one of the province's most unique dining experiences after which you can explore the archaeological dig at the **Colony of Avalon.** Continuing around the peninsula, the next stop is **Cape St. Mary's Ecological Reserve,** and from where it's an easy drive back to St. John's.

Day 3

Head west, stopping at **Trinity,** a tiny fishing village where little has changed in over a century, en route to **Gros Morne National Park,** where during the long days of summer you have time for a walk through the **Tablelands** and can still be at Lobster Cove Head in time to watch the sunset. Gros Morne Cabins are a centrally located base in **Rocky Harbour.**

Day 4

Join a morning boat tour of **Western Brook Pond** and drive north along the Northern Peninsula. Make sure to stop at **Port au Choix National Historic Site** and the **thrombolites of Flowers Cove** en route to Southwest

Green Gardens in Gros Morne National Park

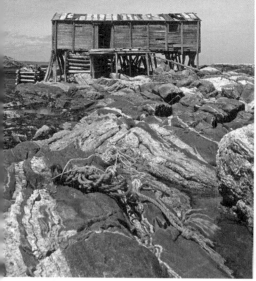

Battle Harbour

Point Amour Lighthouse

Pond Cabins in **L'Anse aux Meadows.** Dinner at the Norseman Restaurant is a must.

Day 5

Visit **L'Anse aux Meadows National Historic Site,** then drive to St. Barbe and put your feet up for a couple of hours on the ferry crossing to Labrador. **Red Bay National Historic Site** should definitely be on your afternoon itinerary, as should the lighthouse at **L'Anse Amour.**

Day 6

Continue north along the Labrador Straits to Mary's Harbour. Park your vehicle and pack an overnight bag for the short boat trip to **Battle Harbour,** an "outport" (remote fishing village) that was abandoned in the 1960s, but where restoration efforts include a restaurant and an inn.

Day 7

Return to the mainland and catch the ferry back to St. Barbe. Stretch your legs at **Marble Mountain,** and continue south to Port-aux-Basques and then home (or catch an evening ferry to Nova Scotia).

St. John's and the Avalon Peninsula

Sights 16

Recreation 24

Entertainment and Events 25

Shopping 27

Food 28

Accommodations
  and Camping 30

Information and Services 33

Getting There and Around 33

Avalon Peninsula 35

S
t. John's, the provincial capital, is a colorful and comfortable city. Situated on the steep inland side of St. John's Harbour, the city's rooftops form a tapestry:

Some are gracefully drawn with swooping mansard curves, some are pancake-flat or starkly pitched, and others are pyramidal with clay pots placed atop the central chimneys. Against this otherwise picture-perfect tapestry, the tangle of electrical wires strung up and down the hillside is a visual offense.

Contrasts of color are everywhere. House windows are framed in deep turquoise, red, bright yellow, or pale pink and are covered with starched white lace curtains. Window boxes are stuffed to overflowing with red geraniums and purple and pink petunias. Along the streets, cement walls brace the hillside, and any blank surface serves as an excuse for a pastel-painted mural. The storefronts on Water Street, as individual as their owners, stand out in Wedgwood blue, lime green, purple, and rose. At street-side, public telephone booths are painted the bright red of old-time fire hydrants.

As the Newfoundlanders say, St. John's offers the best for visitors—another way of saying that Newfoundland is "for someshort on cities and long on coastal outports. But without question, St. John's thrives with places for dining, nightlife, sightseeing, and lodging—more than anywhere else across the island and Labrador. Simply put, the Newfoundlanders have carved a contemporary, livable, and intriguing niche in one of North America's most ancient ports. Come to St. John's for some of Atlantic Canada's most abundant high-quality shopping, unusual dining in lush surroundings, interesting maritime history displayed in fine museums, rousing nightlife and music, and an emerging and eclectic fine-arts scene.

When you're done with the city, there's the rest of the Avalon Peninsula to discover. Within day-tripping distance of downtown, you can go whale-watching at Witless Bay Ecological Reserve, watch archaeologists at work at Ferryland, walk in to North America's most accessible bird sanctuary at Cape St. Mary's, and drive through delightfully named villages like Heart's Desire.

Previous: St. John's Harbour; Gower Street is lined with colorful homes. **Above:** Witless Bay.

Look for ★ to find recommended sights, activities, dining, and lodging.

Highlights

★ **The Rooms:** With a museum, an art gallery, and spectacular harbor views, this magnificent complex showcases the very best of everything in Newfoundland and Labrador (page 16).

★ **Signal Hill:** The sweeping ocean and city views alone make the drive to the top of Signal Hill worthwhile (page 19).

★ **Johnson Geo Centre:** Descend underground in a glass-sided elevator to see the ancient geological world of the province comes to life (page 19).

★ **Quidi Vidi:** With its charming fishing shacks and rugged shoreline, this lake feels remote—but downtown is just over the hill (page 20).

★ **Witless Bay Ecological Reserve:** Jump aboard a tour boat and head out to this reserve, where you're almost guaranteed whale, puffin, and seal sightings (page 37).

★ **Colony of Avalon:** This ongoing archaeological dig is slowly uncovering one of North America's oldest European settlements (page 38).

★ **Cape St. Mary's Ecological Reserve:** Even if you have no real interest in birds, the sights and sounds of thousands of gannets on this offshore rock stack are a spectacle to remember (page 41).

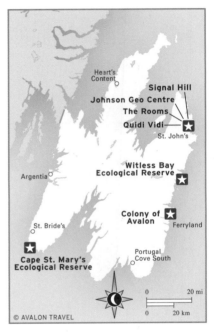

St. John's and the Avalon Peninsula

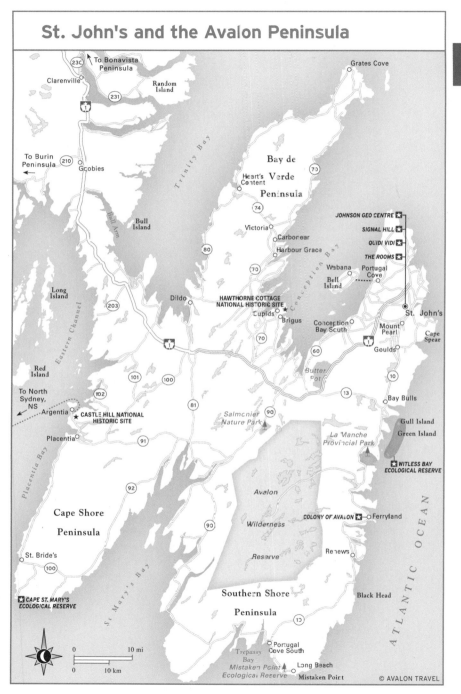

To Bonavista Peninsula

Grates Cove

Clarenville

Random Island

23C

231

1

To Burin Peninsula

210

Gobies

Bull Arm

Trinity Bay

Bay de Verde Peninsula

Heart's Content

Victoria

Carbonear

Harbour Grace

70

74

80

70

JOHNSON GEO CENTRE

SIGNAL HILL

QUIDI VIDI

THE ROOMS

Wabana

Bell Island

Portugal Cove

Conception Bay

Long Island

203

Eastern Channel

Dildo

Cupids

Brigus

HAWTHORNE COTTAGE NATIONAL HISTORIC SITE

Conception Bay South

Mount Pearl

St. John's

Cape Spear

70

1

60

Goulds

Red Island

101

100

To North Sydney, NS

102

Argentia

CASTLE HILL NATIONAL HISTORIC SITE

Placentia

91

81

92

Butter Pot

13

10

Bay Bulls

Gull Island

Green Island

WITLESS BAY ECOLOGICAL RESERVE

Salmonier Nature Park

90

La Manche Provincial Park

Placentia Bay

Cape Shore Peninsula

St. Bride's

100

90

Avalon

Wilderness

Reserve

COLONY OF AVALON

Ferryland

Renews

St Mary's Bay

CAPE ST. MARY'S ECOLOGICAL RESERVE

Southern Shore Peninsula

Black Head

ATLANTIC OCEAN

13

Portugal Cove South

Trepassy Bay

Long Beach

Mistaken Point Ecological Reserve

Mistaken Point

0   10 mi

0   10 km

© AVALON TRAVEL

St. John's

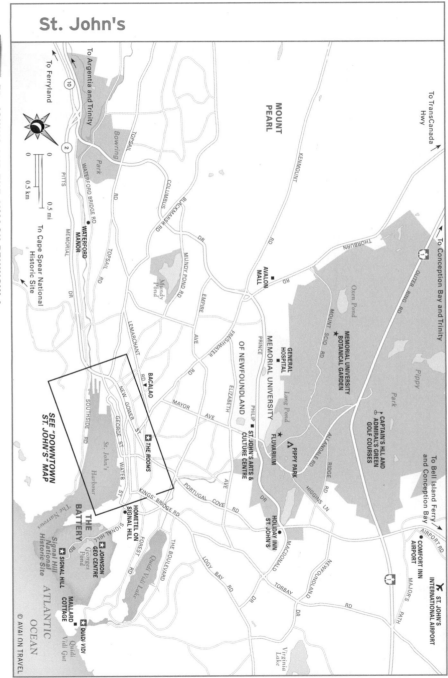

PLANNING YOUR TIME

Whether you arrive by air, by ferry, or overland from the west, St. John's is a definite destination in itself. It has all the amenities of a major city, including top-notch accommodations, a good range of restaurants, and lively nightlife. Sightseeing will easily fill two days, with at least a few hours spent at **The Rooms,** a museum and art gallery complex as good as any in Canada. Don't miss the drive up to **Signal Hill National Historic Site,** and stop at **Johnson Geo Centre** along the way. The **Fluvarium** is a good rainy-day diversion. While the village of **Quidi Vidi** provides a taste of the rest of the province without leaving city limits, the rest of the Avalon Peninsula is well worth exploring.

The options are relatively straightforward—either use St. John's as a base for day trips or plan on an overnight excursion. Two highlights—a whale-watching trip to **Witless Bay Ecological Reserve** and a visit to the historic **Colony of Avalon**—can easily be combined into a day trip. Bird-rich **Cape St. Mary's Ecological Reserve** is also within a couple of hours' drive of St. John's, although if you're arriving by ferry from Nova Scotia, it's only a short detour from the main route into town. If you're arriving by air, five days is the minimum amount of time to allow for exploring the city and the Avalon Peninsula. If you're arriving by ferry with your own vehicle, plan on spending three days on the Avalon Peninsula (including St. John's) and seven days traveling through the central and western portion of the province to the ferry terminal at Port-aux-Basques. Add two days' travel from Halifax (including the two ferry trips from and to Sydney) and you can create a 12-day itinerary with no backtracking.

HISTORY

St. John's officially dates to 1497, when Newfoundlanders say the explorer John Cabot sailed into the harbor and claimed the area for England. By the early 1540s, St. John's Harbour was a major port on old-world maps, and the French explorer Jacques Cartier anchored there for ship repairs. The British—who arrived, conquered, and remained for centuries—have had the greatest impact here. By 1528 the port had its first residence, and the main lanes were the Lower Path (Water Street) and Upper Path (Duckworth Street) Fishing thrived, but settlement was slow. Early on, the defenseless port was easy game for other European imperialists, and in 1665 the Dutch plundered the town. Nevertheless, by 1675, St. John's had a population of 185, as well as 155 cattle and 48 boats anchored at 23 piers. By 1696, the French emerged as England's persistent adversary. The French launched destructive attacks on St. John's in 1696, 1705, and 1709.

St. John's was a seamy port through most of its early years. In a town bereft of permanent settlement and social constraints, 80 taverns and innumerable brothels flourished on Water Street, with a few stores on Duckworth Street and Buckleys Lane (George Street). The port's inhabitants were a motley mix of Spaniards, Portuguese, French, and British; as the latter gained dominance, Anglo immigration was encouraged. In 1892, a huge fire destroyed the city from Water Street to the East End, leveling 1,572 houses and 150 stores and leaving 1,900 families homeless. The stores, commercial buildings, and merchant mansions were re-created in Gothic Revival and Second Empire styles.

The Newfoundland Dog and Labrador Retriever

statues of a Labrador retriever and a Newfoundland dog located in Harbourside Park

The large, long-haired Newfoundland dog is believed to have originated with the early Portuguese, who brought mountain sheepdogs across the Atlantic with them. Considered one of North America's finest show dogs, the Newfoundland is better known locally as a working dog. Its swimming prowess, used to rescue shipwrecked fishers and sailors from stormy seas, has inspired local legends.

Contrary to the name, the Labrador retriever originated on the island of Newfoundland as a descendant of the Newfoundland dog. The retriever was known as the "lesser Newfoundland," "St. John's dog," or "St. John's water dog" until its debut in London at the English Kennel Club in 1903.

Sights

Most of St. John's best sightseeing revolves around the city's long and colorful history. In addition to traditional sights such as The Rooms (the provincial museum) and national historic sites, go beyond the ordinary and plan on sipping a pint of beer at the Crow's Nest and joining a guided walking tour of downtown—both excellent ways to soak up the seafaring ambience of this historic city.

DOWNTOWN

Although adding to the charm in many ways, the layout of downtown defies modern logic. The streets follow footpaths laid out by European fishermen and sailors centuries ago, when towns were not planned but simply evolved for everyone's convenience. Water Street (one of North America's oldest streets) and the other main streets rise parallel to the waterfront and are intersected by roads meandering across the hillside. Historic stone staircases climb grades too steep for paved roads.

★ The Rooms

One of Canada's finest cultural facilities, **The Rooms** (9 Bonaventure Ave., 709/757-8000,

Downtown St. John's

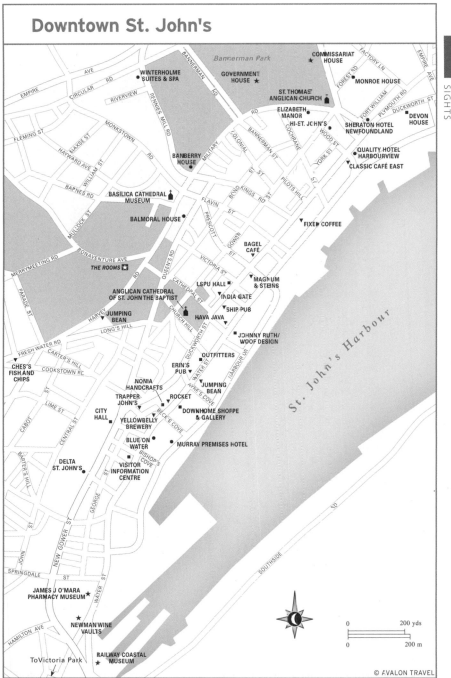

Bannerman Park

★ COMMISSARIAT HOUSE

WINTERHOLME SUITES & SPA

GOVERNMENT HOUSE ★

MONROE HOUSE

ST. THOMAS ANGLICAN CHURCH

ELIZABETH MANOR

HI-ST. JOHN'S

SHERATON HOTEL NEWFOUNDLAND

DEVON HOUSE

BANBERRY HOUSE

QUALITY HOTEL HARBOURVIEW

CLASSIC CAFÉ EAST

BASILICA CATHEDRAL MUSEUM

BALMORAL HOUSE

FIXED COFFEE

BAGEL CAFÉ

BONAVENTURE AVE

THE ROOMS ★

MAGNUM & STEINS

ANGLICAN CATHEDRAL OF ST. JOHN THE BAPTIST

LSPU HALL

INDIA GATE

SHIP PUB

JUMPING BEAN

HAVA JAVA

JOHNNY RUTH/ WOOF DESIGN

St. John's Harbour

OUTFITTERS

CHES'S FISH AND CHIPS

ERIN'S PUB

JUMPING BEAN

NONIA HANDCRAFTS

TRAPPER JOHN'S

ROCKET

CITY HALL

DOWNHOME SHOPPE & GALLERY

YELLOWBELLY BREWERY

BLUE ON WATER

MURRAY PREMISES HOTEL

DELTA ST. JOHN'S

VISITOR INFORMATION CENTRE

JAMES J O'MARA PHARMACY MUSEUM ★

NEWMAN WINE VAULTS ★

To Victoria Park

RAILWAY COASTAL MUSEUM ★

0   200 yds

0   200 m

© AVALON TRAVEL

June-mid-Sept. Mon.-Sat. 10am-5pm, Sun. noon-5pm, mid-Sept.-May Wed.-Sat. 10am-5pm, Sun. noon-5pm, adult $10, senior $6.50, child $5) combines a provincial museum, art gallery, and archives under one roof. Styled on the simple oceanfront "fishing rooms" where Newfoundlanders would process their catch, this complex setting on the site of a 1750s fort is anything but basic. From a distance, it is nothing short of spectacular to see the ultra-modern "rooms" rising above the rest of the city like a mirage. The interior is no less impressive, with huge windows allowing uninterrupted views across the city and harbor. Displays in the museum component encompass the entire natural and human history of Newfoundland and Labrador, from glaciation to modern-day cultural diversity. The art gallery spreads across two floors. More than 7,000 works of art are displayed, with touring exhibits adding to the artistic mix. If you're a history buff with time to spare, include a visit to the archives, which contain more than 500,000 historical photos, plus government and shipping records, maps and atlases, family histories, and personal diaries.

The Rooms is St. John's premier cultural attraction.

Basilica Cathedral Museum

The early Roman Catholics aimed to make an impact on the skyline of St. John's, and did so in the mid-1800s with the **Basilica Cathedral of St. John the Baptist** (200 Military Rd., 709/754-2170, http://thebasilica.ca, June-Sept. Mon.-Fri. 8am-5pm, Sat. 8am-5pm, Sun. 8am-12:30pm, free), one block toward downtown from The Rooms. The Romanesque cathedral, built of stone and shaped like a Latin cross with twin 43-meter-high towers, is now a national historic site. In addition to the museum, guided tours point out the ornate ceilings embellished with gold leaf, numerous statues, and other features.

Anglican Cathedral of St. John the Baptist

The **Anglican Cathedral of St. John the Baptist** (16 Church Hill, 709/726-5677, June Mon.-Fri. 10am-noon and 2pm-4pm, July-Sept. Mon.-Fri. 10am-4pm, Sat. 10am-noon, free) is a national historic site revered by locals (and said to be haunted by a resident ghost). English architect Sir George Gilbert Scott designed the impressive Gothic Revival edifice in Newfoundland bluestone. The cornerstone was laid in 1847, and the Great Fire of 1892 almost gutted the structure. Reconstruction within the walls started the next year. Of special interest are the carved furnishings and sculpted arches, and a gold communion service presented by King William IV.

James J. O'Mara Pharmacy Museum

Inside the splendidly restored and gleaming Art Deco Apothecary Hall, the **James J. O'Mara Pharmacy Museum** (488 Water St., 709/753-5877, Mon.-Fri. 8am-4:30pm, free) recalls a pharmacy of the early 1900s. Apothecary Hall operated as a drug store from 1922 until 1986, but furnishings and equipment on display goes back further, including the oak furniture, which was imported from England in the 1870s.

Newman Wine Vaults

In the late 1700s, wine that had been stored in St. John's was transported back to London, where it was deemed to have a much improved flavor. As a result, a number of wine vaults were constructed in the city, and cases of wine were brought across the Atlantic to mature. The last remaining of these is **Newman Wine Vaults** (436 Water St., 709/739-7870, July-Aug. Tues.-Sat. 10am-4:30pm, adult $6, senior $4, child $3), on the west side of downtown. Ensconced in a more modern shell, the two vaults, held together by mortar from crushed seashells, are the oldest buildings in St. John's.

Railway Coastal Museum

The Newfoundland Railway was a vital link for islanders between 1898 and the last scheduled passenger service in 1969. It extended the length of the island (roughly following the modern-day TransCanada Highway), terminating in the east at what is now the **Railway Coastal Museum** (495 Water St. W., 709/753-5877, summer daily 10am-5pm, fall-spring Tues.-Sun. 10am-5pm, adult $7, senior $6, child $5), west of the New Gower Street overpass. Symbolizing the grandeur of its one-time importance, the city's main railway station forms the backbone of the museum, with historical photographs and memorabilia from days gone by.

Government House

One of few structures that escaped damage in the Great Fire of 1892, **Government House** (50 Military Rd., grounds open daily dawn-dusk) is the residence of the province's lieutenant governor. The impressive 1831 building was constructed of red sandstone quarried from Signal Hill and features a moat, ceiling frescoes, and flower gardens. This, the Commissariat House, and St. Thomas's Anglican Church are on the northern edge of downtown, a steep five-block walk from the waterfront.

Commissariat House

Now protected as a provincial historic site, the three-story **Commissariat House** (11 King's Bridge Rd., 709/729-6370, mid-May-June and Sept.-early Oct. Wed.-Sun. 10am-5pm, July-Aug. daily 10am-5pm, adult $6, senior $4, child $3) began in 1818 as a residence and office for Fort William's assistant commissary general. Over the years, it was used as the St. Thomas's Anglican Church rectory, a nursing home, and a hospital. The interior, furnished with antiques, has been restored in the style of the 1830s.

St. Thomas's Anglican Church

St. Thomas's Anglican Church (corner of King's Bridge Rd. and Military Rd., 709/576-6632, free) is known as the Old Garrison Church. Dating to the 1830s, the city's oldest church houses a cast-iron Hanoverian coat of arms over the door, attesting to the royal lineage. Call for details of summer sanctuary tours.

★ SIGNAL HILL

The distinct geological feature of the **Signal Hill National Historic Site** rises high above the Narrows, at the mouth of St. John's Harbour. On a clear day, it's plainly visible from throughout town, but more importantly, it offers stunning views back across the city, down the coast, and out into the Atlantic Ocean. Although Signal Hill is only a little more than two kilometers from the city center, it's a steep walk, so plan on driving.

★ Johnson Geo Centre

What better place for a geology museum than underground? Access to the **Johnson Geo Centre** (175 Signal Hill Rd., 709/724-7625, daily 9:30am-5pm, adult $12, senior $9, child $6), almost at the top of Signal Hill, is a glass-sided elevator that descends below the rocky landscape to a cavernous room where one entire wall exposes the 550-million-year-old bedrock. Displays describe the entire geological history of the province, from the oldest rocks on earth to modern oil and gas exploration. Highlights include a *Titanic* room, where you can watch footage from exploration of the famous wreck.

Signal Hill National Historic Site

In the 1700s, this hill, once known as the Lookout, served as part of a British signaling system; news of friendly or hostile ships was flagged from Cape Spear to Signal Hill, where the message was conveyed to Fort William in town. In 1762 the Battle of Signal Hill marked the Seven Years' War's final North American land battle, with England victorious and France the loser.

On the road up to the hilltop is the **Visitor Interpretation Centre** (709/772-5367, mid-May-mid-June and Sept.-mid-Oct. Wed.-Sun. 10am-5pm, mid-June-Aug. daily 10am-5pm, adult $4, senior $3.50, child $2), which tells the long and colorful story of Signal Hill through modern and interactive exhibits.

Continuing upward by road or on foot, **Cabot Tower** (mid-Apr.-mid-Nov. daily 9am-5pm, Interpretation Centre admission includes Cabot Tower) is at the very top of Signal Hill. This is where Guglielmo Marconi received the first transatlantic wireless message. The hilltop is pocked with historical remnants. England's Imperial Powder Magazine stored gunpowder during the Napoleonic Wars, and the Queen's Battery—an authentic outport tucked beneath the cliff—guarded the harbor Narrows from 1833.

For hiking, the **North Head Trail** peels off the top of the hill and follows the cliffs to Fort Chain Rock. The **Cuckold's Cove Trail** wends across Signal Hill's leeward side to Quidi Vidi Village.

★ QUIDI VIDI

The Atlantic's watery inroads permeate the St. John's area. Aside from the city's famed harbor, another sizable pocket of the sea— **Quidi Vidi Lake**—lies nearby. Its azure-blue waters meet a boulder-bound coastline, all within the bustling city limits. Quidi Vidi Lake ("kiddie viddie" is the local pronunciation) is best known as the site of the Royal St. John's Regatta, held on the first Wednesday in August. The lake's choppy water also lures windsurfers. Locals enjoy strolls along the grassy banks. To get there, follow Water Street west under Pitts Memorial Drive and turn left onto Route 11 (Blackhead Road).

Beyond the lake is picturesque **Quidi Vidi Village.** Wander the narrow, winding streets

the view from Signal Hill

of this fishing village and you'll never believe a provincial capital lies just over the hill.

Quidi Vidi Battery

Quidi Vidi Battery (Cuckhold's Cove Rd., 709/729-2977, mid-May-Sept. daily 10am-5:30pm, adult $3) sits high on a hill above Quidi Vidi, overlooking the lake and village. The site owes its origin to the French, who built the battery in their effort to capture St. John's in 1762. France lost, and the British took the battery and rebuilt it in 1780. The site has been restored to its War of 1812 glory years, when England fortified the battery in anticipation of an attack by the United States that never materialized. The battery is now staffed by guides dressed in period uniforms of the Royal Artillery.

SOUTH OF DOWNTOWN

Bowring Park

Arguably the city's prettiest, **Bowring Park** has hosted significant guests for many tree-planting ceremonies, including a visit from Queen Elizabeth for the Cabot celebrations in 1997. Crocus and hyacinth beds make a colorful impact during spring, swans glide across the tranquil ponds in summer, and the setting is transformed into a canvas of dappled oranges and reds during autumn. Statues are everywhere, the most famous being of Peter Pan. It's a replica of the original in England's Kensington Gardens, and it serves as a memorial to Sir Edgar Bowring's godchild, who died in an offshore shipwreck.

To get there, stay south on Water Street until the road splits into Waterford Bridge and Topsail Roads; continue on Waterford Bridge Road for three kilometers to the park's entrance.

Cape Spear National Historic Site

The eminently photogenic **Cape Spear National Historic Site lighthouse** (off Rte. 11, 709/772-5367, mid-May-mid-June Wed.-Sun. 10am-6pm, mid-June-early Sept. daily 10am-6pm, early Sept.-mid-Oct. Sat.-Wed. 9am-5pm, adult $4, senior $3.50, child $2) crowns a windy 75-meter-high promontory above the Atlantic Ocean. Built in 1839, the lighthouse ranks as the province's oldest extant beacon and was used until 1955, when the original lighting apparatus was moved to a more efficient building nearby. The keeper's living quarters have been restored, while the adjacent visitors center displays antiques and maritime artifacts.

Quidi Vidi

Outside the lighthouse, the precipitous slopes hold the rusting remains of World War II gun batteries. Hiking trails fan out from the peak. The 10-kilometer trail to Maddox Cove starts here and winds south along the coast, through gullies, bakeapple bogs, and berry patches. If you're lucky, you'll see a family of shy foxes in the high grasses.

The cape, North America's most easterly point, lies six kilometers southeast of St. John's Harbour as the crow flies and 15 kilometers around Route 11's coastal curve. To get there, follow Water Street to the exit for Pitts Memorial Parkway and turn left to Route 11 (Blackhead Road).

PIPPY PARK

Civilization ends and wilderness begins at the **Pippy Park** preserve, which covers 1,343 hectares of woodlands, grasslands, and rolling hills on the steep hilltop plateau overlooking St. John's. In addition to the Fluvarium and the botanical garden, the park is laced with hiking trails and is home to two golf courses. Developed along the rim of the hill, the park fronts Confederation Parkway/Prince Philip Drive and encompasses Memorial University's campus and the government Confederation Building complex. Barrens, marshes, woodlands, ponds, and streams make for a splendid landscape. Moose, muskrats, mink, snowshoe hares, meadow voles, and common shrews roam the hilly terrain, which is studded with balsam fir, spruce, and juniper. The green-winged teal, black and pintail duck, sora rail, American bittern, gyrfalcon, and pied-billed grebe are among the birds lured to Long Pond, the oval lake near the park's edge. Long Pond marks the start of the seven-kilometer Rennies River Trail across the city's hillside to Quidi Vidi Lake.

Fluvarium

The eco-attraction **Fluvarium** (5 Nagle's Pl., 709/754-3474, July-Aug. Mon.-Fri. 9am-5pm, Sat.-Sun. 10am-5pm, Sept.-June Mon.-Fri. 9am-4:30pm, Sat.-Sun. noon-4:30pm, adult $8, senior $6, child $5) overlooks Long Pond from just north of Prince Philip Drive. It's contained in a handsome eight-sided wooden building wrapped with an open porch; you enter on the second floor, a spacious room with ecological exhibits depicting Atlantic salmon and other fish species, marsh birds, and carnivorous plants. The center's pièce de résistance is down a winding stairway. Nine windows pierce the walls and provide spectators a below-water-level look at the brook

Cape Spear

and brown trout, arctic char, and salmon in Nagle's Hill Brook. It's an innovative variation on the traditional aquarium.

Memorial University Botanical Garden

The 38-hectare **Memorial University Botanical Garden** (306 Mt. Scio Rd., 709/737-8590, May-Aug. daily 10am-5pm, Sept.-Nov. daily 10am-4pm, adult $8, senior $6, child $3) is the province's only botanical garden. Garden environments include heather beds, a cottage garden, a rock garden, and a wildflower garden. Hiking trails wind through a boreal forest and a fen, both resplendent with native flowers, shrubs, and trees. The gardens feature a medley of soft colors. Blue forget-me-not, white turtlehead and rhododendron, and pink joe-pye weed bloom among spirea, northern wild raisin, dogwood, and high-bush cranberry. White birch, chokecherry, trembling aspen, ash, willow, and maple surround the botanical medley. To get to the gardens, follow Allandale Road north past Prince Philip Drive and turn west on Mt. Scio Road.

WEST OF DOWNTOWN

Bell Island

One of many islands in Conception Bay, west of St. John's, nine-kilometer-long **Bell Island** has a long history of mining. **No. 2 Mine** (709/488-2880, June-Sept. 10am-6pm, adult $12, senior $10, child $5), which stopped operating in 1949, remains one of the world's most productive submarine (underground) iron ore mines. The striking black-and-white photography of Yousuf Karsh is a highlight of the aboveground museum, while underground the main shaft has been restored and is open for inspection. Guided one-hour tours include the use of a hard hat, but you should bring your own sweater.

Newfoundlanders boast an incredible flair for artistic expression, an ability displayed in the **Bell Island murals.** Large-scale scenes painted on the sides of buildings depict the community's life and people during the ore-mining decades. Look for the half-dozen murals in different locations across the tiny island's northeastern corner, mainly in and near **Wabana,** the largest settlement. One assumes the murals were painted from historical photographs, yet there's a sense of real life to each painting—from a car's black luster to the animated figures and even the clear gleam of a miner's eyes.

To get to Bell Island, follow Route 40 west to Portugal Cove, 15 kilometers from downtown. The ferry (709/895-6931) operates year-round. In summer, sailings are every 20-40 minutes 7am-11:30pm. The fare is $11 per vehicle and driver, plus $5 per additional passenger.

TOURS

Sightseeing Tours

McCarthy's Party (709/579-4480, www.mccarthysparty.com, adult $45, child $25) has been on the sightseeing tour scene for decades. From June to August the company offers daily 2.5-hour guided tours to Signal Hill, Caper Spear, the cathedrals, and other major sites.

Walking Tours

One of many informal walking tours of downtown St. John's is **Boyle's Walking Tours** (709/364-6845, www.boyletours.com, mid-June-mid-Sept.), led by the very prim and proper Sir Cavendish Boyle. The Where They Once Stood tour ($20, cash only) departs Tuesday and Friday at 9:55am from the lobby of the Sheraton Hotel Newfoundland.

The **Haunted Hike** (709/685-3444, www.hauntedhike.com, June-mid-Sept., $10) departs Sunday-Thursday at 9:30pm from the west entrance to the Anglican church at the corner of Duckworth Street and Church Hill. With the Reverend Thomas Wyckham Jarvis leading the way, you'll explore the darkened backstreets learning of murders, mysteries, and ghosts. It's an experience you won't forget in a hurry.

Recreation

Don't let bad weather prevent you from enjoying the outdoors—the locals certainly don't. Sure, it may be foggy or raining, but in many ways this adds to the St. John's experience when you're out hiking or striding the local fairways.

HIKING AND BIKING

The hilly streets of downtown St. John's aren't conducive to walking and biking, but if you're looking for wilderness, you don't need to travel too far from the city. A five-minute drive from downtown is **Pippy Park.** Follow Allendale Road north over the TransCanada Highway and look for the parking area beyond the golf course entrance. From this point, hiking trails loop past numerous lakes and through native forest.

Alongside the TransCanada Highway, 36 kilometers south of downtown, is **Butter Pot Provincial Park** (day pass $5 per vehicle), a 2,800-hectare wilderness of forests, bogs, and barrens—a taste of the interior a 30-minute drive from the city. The name "Butter Pot" is a local term for a rounded hill, many of which occur within the park boundary, including along Butter Pot Hill Trail, a 3.3-kilometer walk to a 300-meter-high summit. Along the way you'll see signs of ancient glacial action, including displaced boulders known as "erratics," while at the summit, hikers are rewarded with views extending north to Bell Island. This trail starts beside Site 58 of the park campground. With minimal elevation gain, the Peter's Pond Trail parallels a small lake from the day-use area; you can turn around after one kilometer or continue to Butter Pot Hill.

SCUBA DIVING

Situated on Atlantic Canada's oldest shipping routes, the St. John's area is incredibly rich in shipwrecks. What's more, the waters here are as clear as the Caribbean—20- to 30-meter visibility is common—and reasonably warm summer-autumn, although a wetsuit is advisable. One of the most accessible wreck-diving sites is **Lance Cove,** on Bell Island, where four iron-ore carriers were torpedoed by German U-boats during World War II. Also in Conception Bay are much older whaling boats and a number of wrecks close enough to be accessible for shore diving. Based at Conception Bay South, **Ocean Quest** (17 Stanley's Rd., 709/834-7234, www.oceanquestadventures. com) takes divers to the bay and other dive sites for a full-day boat charter rate of $245 per person (includes rental gear). This company also operates a dive school and a dive shop, and has a number of packages combining diving with other adventures such as snorkeling with humpback whales.

Entertainment and Events

NIGHTLIFE

It's said St. John's has more pubs, taverns, and bars per capita than anyplace else in Atlantic Canada. Spend any time wandering through downtown after dark and you'll probably agree. The city's international port status is partly the reason. Even better, these watering holes serve double duty as venues for music of various styles, including traditional Newfoundland, folk, Irish, country, rock, and jazz. The website www.georgestreetlive.ca has entertainment listings.

A local band of note is **Great Big Sea,** which combines modern rock and traditional Newfoundland folk to create a sound and atmosphere that draws sellout crowds throughout Canada.

Pubs

The energetic pub scene centers on a one-block stretch of George Street off Water Street. The weekend starts late Friday evening, picks up again on Saturday afternoon, and lasts until 2am (and at some places keeps up through Sunday).

On the corner of George and Water Streets, **YellowBelly Brewery** (288 Water St., 709/757-3780, daily 11am-2am) is ensconced in a five-story building that dates to 1725—one of the city's oldest buildings and one of the few to escape the Great Fire of 1892. A faithful renovation creates an authentic atmosphere for enjoying beers brewed on-site, including unique choices such as Hard Tack Ale, which is made from day-old bread sourced from a local bakery. Ask at the restaurant for a tour of the building.

Among George Street's abundance of pubs and eating establishments, **Trapper John's** (2 George St., 709/579-9630, daily noon-2am) ranks as a city entertainment mainstay, hosting notable provincial folk groups and bands. The patrons will gladly initiate visitors to Newfoundland with a "screech-in" ceremony

for free. **Green Sleeves Pub** (14 George St., 709/579-1070, daily 11am-close) doubles as a weekend hub for traditional, rock, and Irish concerts and jam sessions. **Fat Cat Blues Bar** (5 George St., 709/739-5554, Tues.-Sun. 8pm-3am) presents concerts, open mic, blues rock, and women's jam sessions.

The **Ship Pub** (265 Duckworth St., 709/753-3870, daily noon-2am) is a dimly lit room that has been a venue for local and provincial recording acts for years, and it continues to draw Newfoundland's hottest up-and-coming jazz, blues, and folk musicians each weekend night. These same artists, as well as literary types, are the main customers—you just never know who might be on stage or in the audience.

In the vicinity of the Ship Inn, the **Crow's Nest** (709/753-6927, Tues.-Thurs. 4:30pm-7:30pm, Fri. noon-10pm, Sat. 2pm-8pm) opened in 1942 as a retreat for naval officers, but this once-exclusive club is now open to interested visitors (dress code is "smart casual"). The old-fashioned room is a treasure trove of naval memorabilia, which includes a periscope from a German U-boat that was captured off St. John's during World War II. The club is on the fourth floor of an old brick warehouse between Water and Duckworth Streets; the entrance is opposite the war memorial.

PERFORMING ARTS

The **Resource Centre for the Arts** (LSPU Hall, 3 Victoria St., 709/753-4531, www.rca.nf.ca) stages productions by the resident RCA Theatre Company and also hosts professional touring groups throughout the year. Ticket prices vary depending on the event, but are always reasonable.

The **Arts and Culture Centre** (corner of Allandale Rd. and Prince Philip Dr., 709/729-3900) presents a wide range of theater, music, and dance on its Main Stage, with artists and troupes from across Canada. The center is also home to the **Newfoundland Symphony Orchestra** (709/722-4441, www.nsomusic. ca), which has a September-April season.

FESTIVALS AND EVENTS
Spring

The city shines as a music festival venue. The biggest and best is June's nine-day **Festival 500 Growing the Voices** (709/738-6013, www.growingthevoices.com), held in odd-numbered years. Highlights include the noontime medley of harbor ship horns; city-wide theater, workshops, and dance; and Newfoundland, folk, electronic, jazz, New Age, and African concerts.

Summer

Shakespeare by the Sea Festival (709/722-7287, www.shakespearebytheseafestival.com) takes place for three weeks in July, Friday-Sunday at 6pm. Expect outdoor productions of the Bard's best by the acclaimed Loyal Shakespearean Company. The venues change annually, but may be as dramatic as Cape Spear National Historic Site or as intimate as the Newman Wine Vault.

The **Signal Hill Tattoo** is a tribute to the landmark Battle of Signal Hill that ended the war between the English and French in North America. The military event is staged dramatically, with military drills by foot soldiers, artillery detachments, fife and drum bands, and more. It all takes place up at Signal Hill National Historic Site early July-mid-August on Wednesday, Thursday, Saturday, and Sunday at 11am and 3pm.

Beginning in late July or early August, Prince Edward Plaza on George Street is the outdoor setting for the weeklong **George Street Festival** (www.georgestreetlive.ca), which offers performances by top entertainers. Crowds begin gathering in the afternoon, and by midnight there may be upwards of 8,000 revelers on the street.

"Screeched In"

Newfoundlanders dote on the codfish, and visitors are invited to pledge piscatorial loyalty to King Cod in hilarious induction ceremonies conducted on tours and in touristy restaurants. The tradition dates to the early 1900s, when a visiting U.S. naval officer followed the lead of his St. John's host by downing a glass of rum in one gulp. His reaction to swallowing the unlabeled rum was an undignified screech. And so the tradition was born, as U.S. servicemen docked in St. John's came ashore to sample the "screech."

To be "screeched in" in proper style, a visitor dons fishing garb, downs several quick shots of Screech rum, kisses a cod, joins in singing a local ditty, poses for a photograph, and receives an official certificate. It's strictly tourist nonsense, but visitors love it. Mostly because of its authentic atmosphere, **Trapper John's** (2 George St., 709/579-9630, daily noon-2am) in downtown St. John's is one of the best places to be "screeched in."

The **Royal St. John's Regatta** (709/576-8921, www.stjohnsregatta.org) is a city tradition that officially dates back to 1818 (making it North America's oldest organized sporting event), although it was probably contested as early as the late 1700s. What began as a rowing contest between visiting sailors has morphed into a world-class event drawing rowers from around the world. Held at Quidi Vidi Lake on the first Wednesday in August, the event draws up to 50,000 spectators and is so popular that the city long ago declared the day a civic holiday.

Winter

Most of the winter action centers on **Mile One Centre** (50 New Gower St., 709/576-7657, www.mileonecentre.com), where the St. John's IceCaps hockey franchise competes in the American Hockey League.

Shopping

An abundance of arts and crafts stores can be found in downtown St. John's. Aside from these, east along Duckworth Street beyond downtown is a string of interesting shops specializing in Newfoundland music, pet paraphernalia, and the like. My favorite is **Johnny Ruth** (181 Water St., 709/722-7477, Mon.-Wed. and Sat. 10am-6pm, Thurs.-Fri. 10am-9pm, Sun. noon-5pm), which stocks locally printed shirts by Living Planet that feature a politically incorrect Newfoundland slant.

ARTS AND CRAFTS

Craft shops downtown offer every conceivable craft available, and new developments continually increase the variety. One of the best places to start is **Devon House** (59 Duckworth St., 709/753-2749, Mon.-Sat. 10am-5pm, Sun. noon-5pm), in a historic building below the Sheraton Hotel Newfoundland. An outlet for the Craft Council of Newfoundland and Labrador, it displays an excellent sampling of traditional and contemporary wares.

For designer pieces, check out retail sales outlets in the artists' studios, such as **Woof Design** (181 Water St., 709/722-7555, summer daily 9am-5:30pm), which specializes in mohair, woolen, and angora apparel, plus whalebone carvings and other crafts. Other shops operate as cottage-industry outlets. **Nonia Handcrafts** (286 Water St., 709/753-8062, June-Sept. Mon.-Sat. 10am-5:30pm, Sun.

12:30pm-4pm, the rest of the year Tues.-Sat. 10am-5:30pm) is among the best craft shops, carrying handwoven apparel, weavings, parkas, jewelry, hooked mats, domestic wares, and handmade toys.

Other shops sell a variety of wares: Grenfell parkas from St. Anthony, books about Newfoundland, local Purity-brand candies, tinned biscuits or seafood, bottles of savory spices, pottery and porcelain, handmade copper and tin kettles, model ships, soapstone and stone carvings, fur pelts and rugs, apparel, folk art, and handwoven silk, wool, cotton, and linen. Expect to find most of these goods at the **Downhome Shoppe & Gallery** (303 Water St., 709/722-2970, Mon.-Sat. 10am-6pm, Sun. noon-5pm).

Top-notch private galleries are plentiful. **Christina Parker Gallery** (50 Water St., 709/753-0580, Mon.-Fri. 10am-5:30pm, Sat. 11am-5pm) showcases Newfoundland's avant-garde spectrum; for more traditional art, plan on visiting the **Emma Butler Gallery** (111 George St., 709/739-7111, Tues.-Sat. 11am-5pm).

OUTDOOR GEAR

The Outfitters (220 Water St., 709/579-4453, Mon.-Sat. 10am-6pm, Sun. noon-5pm) sells an excellent range of outdoor wear, including winter jackets. It also has canoes, kayaks, and skis and is a clearinghouse for information about outdoor recreation around the island.

Food

No one would describe the St. John's dining scene as sophisticated, but it is better—by far—than anywhere else in the province. As you might imagine, seafood features prominently on most menus. Cod is a staple, while in better restaurants you'll find Atlantic salmon, mussels, scallops, halibut, and lobster.

CAFÉS AND CHEAP EATS

★ **Jumping Bean** (47 Harvey Rd., 709/754-4538, Mon.-Fri. 7:30am-5pm, Sat.-Sun. 10am-5pm, lunches $7-11) is a quiet, modern place away from the downtown core. The owners are primarily coffee-roasters, so you know you'll be getting the very freshest coffee, but you can also try the most unique flavor in the province—Screech Coffee, which is infused with Newfoundland rum. Jumping Bean also has a downtown location in the **Atlantic Place building** (215 Water St., 709/754-4627, Mon.-Fri. 7am-6pm, Sat.-Sun. 9am-6pm), which is notable for sweeping harbor views and outdoor tables that become prime real estate on warm summer days.

The **Bagel Café** (246 Duckworth St., 709/739-4470, daily 7am-9pm, lunches $7-11) feels more like a restaurant than a coffeehouse. All breakfasts are under $10, including heart-smart options like poached eggs and cereal with low-fat yogurt. Potato bakes make a tasty treat, or order something more substantial, like lasagna.

Continuing along Duckworth away from downtown, you soon come to **Fixed Coffee** (183 Duckworth St., 709/576-7797, Mon.-Fri. 7:30am-8pm, Sat.-Sun. 8am-6pm, lunches $8-14), with a distinct artsy feel. The coffee is as good as anywhere in the province, but it also has delicious chai lattes and hot chocolate. The food menu is ever-changing, but generally includes breakfast sandwiches and wraps, as well as lunchtime salads made from produce sourced from a local farm.

DELIS

Along downtown's busiest street, ★ **Rocket** (272 Water St., 709/738-2011, daily 7:30am-9pm, lunches $8-13) is a deli with a difference. It stocks all the goodies you would expect to

Head to Rocket for delicious cooking in a casual atmosphere.

find in a Newfoundland deli, as well as bakery and lunch items, soups and sandwiches, and a huge selection of teas and coffees. Many customers pick up their orders and move on to the adjacent room, which is not really a restaurant but somewhere to simply sit down and eat lunch.

The lower end of Freshwater Road has a concentration of bakeries and delicatessens. **Stockwood's Bakery and Delicatessen** (316 Freshwater Rd., 709/726-2083, 24 hours daily) stocks fresh sandwiches, cold plates, salads, cakes, and baking supplies and is never closed. For a selection of fancier cakes and pastries, stop by **Manna European Bakery & Deli** (342 Freshwater Rd., 709/739-6992, daily 7am-7pm).

Head to the **Seafood Shop** (7 Rowan St., Churchill Sq., 709/753-1153, Mon.-Sat. 9:30am-5:30pm) for fresh and packaged seafood such as cod, shrimp, halibut, mussels, and scallops.

For a tantalizing overview of Newfoundland cuisine, head to ★ **Bidgoods** (Rte. 10, Goulds, 709/368-3125, Mon.-Sat. 9am-7pm, Sun. 10am-6pm), on the south side of the city. This 50-year-old store stocks every taste sensation known to the province, including seal flipper pie, caribou, salted fish, salmon, and cod tongues and cheeks. Not much is prepackaged here, but the produce (especially west coast strawberries), berry preserves, shellfish, smoked and pickled fish, and sweet tea biscuits make delicious picnic additions.

PUB GRUB

In the heart of downtown, **YellowBelly Brewery** (288 Water St., 709/757-3780, daily 11am-2am, $15-28) is best known as one of Canada's best brewpubs, but it also serves up excellent food, with dishes such as Drunken Salmon using beer brewed in-house as a prime ingredient. The menu of wood-fired pizzas includes choices such as the Costa Rican—ham, pineapple, coconut, and banana peppers.

The **Ship Pub** (265 Duckworth St., 709/753-3870, food service daily noon-3pm,

lunches $7.50-13) is a cozy neighborhood pub best known for its live music, but you can order simple lunches from the inexpensive blackboard menu.

REGIONAL CUISINE

"Newfoundland cuisine" revolves around seafood, and traditionally it's been deep-fried, which is often bemoaned by outsiders not used to this style of cooking. That said, it's worth trying fish-and-chips at least once—and not at a regular family restaurant, but somewhere it is a specialty, such as **Ches's Fish and Chips** (9 Freshwater Rd., 709/726-2373, daily 11am-6pm, $9-16). Here, tender deep-fried fillets and crisp french fries are served in an atmosphere of Formica and bright lights.

Walk a few blocks east of downtown to reach **Classic Café East** (73 Duckworth St., 709/579-4444, Sun.-Tues. 8am-2:30pm, Wed.-Sat. 8am-9pm, $13-21), a popular spot that gets crowded with all types who come seeking delicious seafood chowder, cod tongues with scrunchions, and other traditional Newfoundland fare at moderate prices in a cozy atmosphere. For dessert, try the spotted dick (a traditional steamed pudding) or the cheesecake with partridgeberry sauce.

A huge step up in style and price, but still rooted in traditional cooking, is **Bacalao** (65 LeMarchant Rd., 709/579-6565, Tues.-Sun. noon-2:30pm and 6pm-9:30pm, $19-33), which means "salt cod" in Spanish. Within a stylish setting, top chefs serve up Newfoundland's best-known export, cod, in a number of creative ways, using local, organic ingredients whenever possible. The local theme extends through many dishes—mussels are steamed open in Quidi Vidi beer, and the caribou salad is drizzled with blueberry wine from the province's only winery. As an entrée, the salted cod poached in olive oil and accompanied by smoked and braised pork belly is hard to fault, or choose dishes such as seafood risotto and Game of the Day (it was caribou with partridgeberry sauce last time I visited). Save room for a slice of patriotic Republic

Mousse, which is decorated in the three colors of the Newfoundland flag.

I've saved the best for last. If you are looking for the combination of creative local cooking within one of North America's oldest wooden buildings, plan on dining at ★ **Mallard Cottage** (8 Barrows Rd., Quidi Vidi, 709/237-7314, Tues. 5:30pm-9pm, Wed.-Sat. 10am-2pm and 5pm-9:30pm, Sun. 10am-5pm, $22-34). Located in the fishing village of Quidi Vidi, a five-minute drive north of downtown, the national historic site-protected building has undergone extensive renovations to create a homey and welcoming ambience. But it is the food itself that is the main draw. The menu changes daily (check their website www.mallardcottage.ca) and is always filled with local, seasonal game, seafood, and produce. Generally, seafood and pork dishes dominate the menu; the restaurant also has regular special events, such as lobster boils, outdoor barbecues, live music on Sunday afternoons, and one dish in particular that garners international attention each spring—seal burgers.

CONTEMPORARY

The chic industrial-style signage out front is a giveaway—**Magnum & Steins** (329 Duckworth St., 709/576-6500, Sun.-Thurs. 5:30pm-10pm, Fri.-Sat. 5:30pm-11pm, $28-45) is clearly unlike any other restaurant in the city. If you're looking for a traditional Newfoundland experience, eat elsewhere. If you're looking for creative city-style cooking and top-notch presentation, this place is a welcome break from deep-fried seafood. Sunday-Wednesday, a three-course dinner is $55 per person.

Blue on Water (319 Water St., 709/754-2583, daily for breakfast, lunch, and dinner, $30-46) is a smallish modern space with a bright atmosphere. Modern cooking is combined with traditional foods in dishes such as kippered mackerel baked with cream and shallots. Lunches include gourmet sandwiches and a delicious seafood bouillabaisse. In the evening, things get serious (and expensive) with starters like shrimp in a coconut tempura and spicy pineapple chutney and mains like salmon stuffed with roasted red peppers and spinach. The wine list covers all bases.

East Indian

Fine East Indian cuisine can be found at **India Gate** (286 Duckworth St., 709/753-6006, Mon.-Fri. 11:30am-1:30pm and 5pm-9:30pm, Sat.-Sun. 5pm-9:30pm, $12-20). The extensive menu includes tandoori dishes; prawns, lamb, beef, and chicken cooked in the masala, korma, and vindaloo styles; and a wide array of vegetarian entrées. Prices are inexpensive to moderate, portions are generous, and the atmosphere is quiet and relaxed.

Accommodations and Camping

While St. John's may not have a huge selection of budget accommodations, it does provide an excellent choice of historic B&Bs that offer excellent value. A few major chains are represented downtown (and are also well priced), while you'll find all the familiar chains along major arteries. As elsewhere in Atlantic Canada, demand for rooms is highest in summer, and you should make reservations far in advance. While the larger downtown properties supply parking, at smaller properties you may be expected to use metered street parking.

DOWNTOWN
Under $50

Ensconced in one of the city's famously photogenic pastel-colored townhouses is **HI-St. John's** (8 Gower St., 709/754-4789, www.hihostels.ca), an affiliate of Hostelling International. Within walking distance of downtown, dorm rooms are spacious and

Hometel on Signal Hill

A restored Queen Anne-style townhouse, the **Balmoral House** (38 Queen's Rd., 709/754-5721 or 877/428-1055, www.balmoralhouse.com, $139-179 s or d) offers four large guest rooms, each with a fireplace, a private bath, antique furnishings, a TV, Internet access, and an expansive view of the harbor. Rates include a full breakfast and use of off-street parking.

If you're traveling with children and want to stay downtown, **Quality Hotel-Harbourview** (2 Hill O'Chips, 709/754-7788 or 800/228-5151, www.stjohnsqualityhotel.com, from $149 s or d) is a good choice. It has 162 midsize rooms, a popular restaurant overlooking the harbor, free outdoor parking, and free local calls. Rooms with harbor views start at $165, but check online for deals.

$150-200

Take a break from the city's abundant historic accommodations by reserving one of the spacious rooms at ★ **Hometel on Signal Hill** (10 St. Joseph's Ln., 709/739-7799 or 866/739-7799, www.hometels.ca, $160-210 s or d). Located near the base of Signal Hill but still an easy stroll to downtown, this newer lodging fills a row of modern townhouses, each containing up to eight guest rooms. The styling is contemporary throughout, with comfortable beds and large bathrooms adding to the appeal. A light breakfast is included in the rates, with guests congregating in a dining room above the lobby to fill themselves with toast, cereal, and fresh muffins.

Instead of a hotel with a restaurant, **Blue on Water** (319 Water St., 709/754-2583 or 877/431-2583, www.blueonwater.com, from $189 s or d) is a restaurant with 12 upstairs rooms. Like the Hometel on Signal Hill, it offers a modern ambience but is more centrally located. The decor is slick and contemporary—think 400-thread-count sheets, high-speed Internet connections, and flat-screen TVs. On the downside, the nearest parking is a public lot behind the property, there is no elevator, and check-in is within the restaurant.

come with a maximum of four beds. Other facilities include a well-equipped kitchen, a small backyard with a barbecue, and wireless Internet. Rates are $30 for members and $35 nonmembers. The double rooms are $75-85 and $85-89, respectively.

$100-150

Opposite Bannerman Park, **Elizabeth Manor** (21 Military Rd., 709/753-7733 or 888/263-3786, www.elizabethmanor.nl.ca, $129-229 s or d) was built in 1894, following the Great Fire of 1892. Completely revamped in 2004, it now offers nine spacious en suite guest rooms, a sundeck, and a library with art and books about the province. Rates include a full breakfast.

Waterford Manor (185 Waterford Bridge Rd., 709/754-4139, www.thewaterfordmanor.com, $135-275 s or d), a beautiful Queen Anne-style mansion near Bowring Park, is furnished with antiques of the late 19th century. The seven guest rooms vary greatly in size, but all have TVs and en suite bathrooms.

But once you're in your room, you'll think you're paying a lot more than you really are.

Backing onto Bannerman Park and with a beautiful rear garden, ★ **Banberry House** (116 Military Rd., 709/579-8006 or 877/579-8226, www.banberryhouse.com, $159 s or d) oozes style throughout. My favorite of five guest rooms is the Labrador Room, which is filled with stylish mahogany furniture (including a work desk) and has a super-comfortable bed, a four-piece bath, and garden views. Rates include a full Newfoundland breakfast.

Across the road from the heart of the downtown waterfront, a row of 1846 wooden warehouses has been transformed into **Murray Premises Hotel** (5 Becks Cove, 709/738-7773 or 866/738-7773, www.murraypremiseshotel.com, $199-259 s or d). The 67 rooms fill the top two floors and an adjacent wing. Each is super spacious and features luxurious touches such as maple furniture, heated towel racks and jetted tubs in the oversized bathrooms, and TV/DVD combos. In-room coffee, complimentary newspapers, and free wireless Internet add to the appeal.

Closer to the airport than to the waterfront, the **Holiday Inn St. John's** (180 Portugal Cove Rd., 709/722-0506 or 800/933-0506, www.ihg.com, $175 s or d) is handy to Pippy Park, Memorial University, and the Confederation Building complex. The hotel offers 256 guest rooms, an indoor pool and waterslide, an up-to-date fitness center, a restaurant and lounge, a laundry, and a business center. Outside of the summer season, check online for rooms around $120.

Over $200

Sheraton Hotel Newfoundland (115 Cavendish Sq., 709/726-4980 or 800/325-3535, www.starwoodhotels.com, from $250 s or d) has an auspicious location, on the former site of Fort William. The first Hotel Newfoundland, one of the Canadian Pacific's deluxe properties, opened in 1925. After many years' service, it was demolished to make room for this handsome hotel. Opened in 1982, the hillside property has more than 300 guest rooms, free parking, and a contemporary restaurant, lounge, fitness center (with an indoor pool, table tennis, squash courts, sauna, and whirlpool), and shopping arcade with a hairdresser.

Delta St. John's (120 New Gower St., 709/739-6404 or 888/890-3222, www.deltahotels.com, from $260 s or d) is an avant-garde high-rise that offers more than 400 rooms and suites; restaurants and a pub; fitness facilities that include an indoor heated pool, exercise equipment, a whirlpool, a sauna, and squash courts; a shopping arcade; and covered parking.

AIRPORT
$100-150

Comfort Inn Airport (106 Airport Rd., 709/753-3500, www.comfortinnstjohns.com, $129-149 s or d) is conveniently located across from St. John's International Airport and features 100 rooms and suites, a restaurant and lounge, a business center, a fitness center, airport transfers, and free continental breakfast.

CAMPGROUNDS

Pippy Park Campground (Nagle's Pl., 709/737-3669, www.pippypark.com, May-Sept., $30-45), 2.5 kilometers northwest of downtown, fills on a first-come, first-served basis. It offers more than 150 sites, most of which are private and well spaced. Amenities include a general store, a playground, wireless Internet (in only one section of the campground), and picnic shelters. The Fluvarium (great for children) is across the road, while trails lead from the campground to all corners of Pippy Park.

Butter Pot Provincial Park, along the TransCanada Highway, 36 kilometers south of downtown, has a 126-site campground open late May-late Sept. The cost is $28 per night, with showers and laundry facilities provided. Each private site has a fire pit and picnic table. Activities include hiking and water sports such as lake swimming and canoeing (rentals available). Three playgrounds will keep the young ones occupied.

Farther out, but in a beautiful lakeside location, ★ **La Manche Provincial Park** (Rte. 10, late May-late Sept., $18-28) has 83 campsites spread around two forested loops. Although there are no showers or hookups, the facility fills every summer weekend. In addition to kayaking and fishing, campers take advantage of trails leading along La Manche River and down to an abandoned fishing village. Reservations for Butter Pot Provincial Park and La Manche Provincial Park can be made by calling 877/214-2267 or online at www.nlcamping.ca.

Information and Services

Tourist Information

The **provincial tourism office** (709/729-2830 or 800/563-6353, www.newfoundlandlabrador.com) and **Destination St. John's** (709/739-8899 or 877/739-8899, www.destinationstjohns.com) are both good sources of information when planning your trip.

There's an **information booth** at the airport (open whenever flights are arriving) and another just beyond the ferry dock at Argentia (open for all ferry arrivals). When you get downtown, search out the **City of St. John's Visitor Information Centre** (348 Water St., 709/576-8106, www.stjohns.ca, May-early Oct. daily 10am-4:30pm, early Oct.-Apr. Mon.-Fri. 10am-4:30pm), in a three-story red-brick building by the Delta St. John's.

Health and Safety

Local hospitals under the jurisdiction of Eastern Health include the **General Hospital** (300 Prince Philip Dr., 709/737-6335), **Janeway Children's Health Centre** (also at 300 Prince Phillip Dr., 709/778-4228), and **St. Clare's Mercy Hospital** (154 LeMarchant Rd., 709/777-5501).

The **Royal Newfoundland Constabulary** (911 or 709/729-8333) deals with police matters within city limits, while the **Royal Canadian Mounted Police** (709/772-5400) protect the rest of the province.

Getting There and Around

Even though St. John's sits on the far eastern edge of the North American continent, it is a transportation hub for air travel through the province and for shipping routes across the Atlantic Ocean.

GETTING THERE
Air

St. John's International Airport (www.stjohnsairport.com) is off Portugal Cove Road, a simple 15-minute drive northwest from downtown. The airport is a large modern facility, with ATMs, a currency exchange center, an information booth (open daily until the arrival of the last flight), a restaurant and lounge, a duty-free shop, a newsstand, and car rental desks for all the major companies (Avis, Budget, Discount, Hertz, National, and Thrifty). Taxis charge a flat rate to any of the major downtown hotels: $32 for the first person, $6 each additional person.

St. John's is served by direct **Air Canada** (709/726-7880 or 888/247-2262) flights from Halifax, Montréal, and Toronto, with connections made through these three cities from its worldwide network. **WestJet** (888/937-8538) uses Halifax as its eastern hub, from where regular connections can be made to St. John's. Local airlines include **PAL Airlines** (709/576-3943 or 800/563-2800, www.palairlines.com), with flights between Halifax and St. John's, plus onward flights throughout the province, and **Air Saint-Pierre** (902/873-3566, www.airsaintpierre.com), with daily shuttle services to the St-Pierre and Miquelon Islands.

Car

If you are coming by car from the mainland, you need to get to Sydney, Nova Scotia. From here, two ferry routes cross to Newfoundland. The longer and more expensive option is to catch the ferry from Sydney to Argentia. Taking this route, you are left with a much shorter drive upon reaching Newfoundland. Downtown St. John's is 134 kilometers northeast of Argentia via Route 100 and Route 1.

The alternative is to catch the ferry from Sydney to Port-aux-Basques, a short trip, but one that leaves you with a 900-kilometer (11-hour) drive across the province to St. John's via the TransCanada Highway.

From Halifax, it's 430 kilometers to Sydney, so allow around 22 hours, inclusive of either ferry crossing, to reach St. John's.

Ferry

One of two ferry services to Newfoundland from North Sydney (Nova Scotia) docks at **Argentia,** a 134-kilometer drive southwest of St. John's. Ferries are operated by **Marine Atlantic** (709/227-2431 or 800/341-7981, www.marineatlantic.ca, adult $125, senior $115, child $62, from $253 for vehicles) two times weekly mid-June-late September (at other times of year, you will need to use the Sydney to Port-aux-Basques route). The trip over from the mainland takes 14 hours; dorm beds and cabins are available.

Bus

There is no bus service between the ferry terminal at Argentia and St. John's. For those arriving in Newfoundland via the ferry to Port-aux-Basques, **DRL-LR** (709/263-2171, www.drl-lr.com) operates daily long-haul bus service to St. John's (14 hours, $126 one-way).

GETTING AROUND

Locals complain that downtown parking space is scarce. Not so, the city says, countering that there are 1,500 parking slots at the Municipal Parking Garage on Water Street, other downtown garages, and on the streets. Some 800 street spaces are metered for loonies (the $1 coin) and quarters; when the time is up, the cops are quick to ticket expired meters.

Bus

Metrobus (709/570-2020, www.metrobus.com, adult $2.25, child $1.75 per sector) operates an extensive bus network that leads from downtown to all outer suburbs. Transfers are valid for 90 minutes of travel in one direction.

Taxi

Cabs wait at the airport ($32 to downtown for one person, then $6 each additional) and also out front of major hotels like the Delta St. John's and Sheraton Hotel Newfoundland. Travel within downtown runs $6-10. Major companies include **City Wide** (709/722-0003), **Jiffy** (709/722-2222), and **Co-op** (709/726-6666).

Car and RV Rental

All major car rental companies are represented in St. John's, but check local restrictions, such as bans on traveling to certain parts of the island and along the TransLabrador Highway.

During July and August, **Islander RV** (709/738-7368 or 888/848-2267, www.islanderrv.com) charges $250 per day for a two-person camper and from $305 for an RV that sleeps six. Per day, 150 free kilometers are included, and a seven-day minimum rental is required during summer. Rental rates drop to $180-215 per day in the shoulder seasons.

Avalon Peninsula

If sightseeing time is short and you must bypass the rest of Newfoundland, consider the Avalon Peninsula as a manageable stand-in. Although it is known by a single name, it is actually four peninsulas, two jutting southward and two northward. The city of St. John's sprawls across one. The highlights of the remaining three are covered in this section.

BACCALIEU TRAIL

This route hugs the northern Avalon coastline, winding around Conception Bay to the town of Carbonear and then looping south along the east side of Trinity Bay back to the TransCanada Highway. The loop makes an ideal full-day trip from St. John's (around 380 kilometers), but accommodations en route may tempt you to stay longer.

Brigus

Picturesque Brigus lies across Conception Bay from Conception Bay South, or around a 50 minutes' drive via the TransCanada Highway and Route 63. The town's most famous native son, Captain Robert Bartlett, was an Arctic explorer who accompanied Robert Peary on his 1908 North Pole expedition. Bartlett's 1820 house is now **Hawthorne Cottage National Historic Site** (corner of South St. and Irishtown Rd., 709/528-4004, mid-May-late June and early Sept.-early Oct. Wed.-Sun. 9:30am-5:30pm, late June-early Sept. daily 9am-6pm, adult $5, senior $4.50, child $3). Built in 1830, the cottage is a rare intact example of the *cottage orné* (decorative) style, with interpretive panels dotting the gardens telling the stories of Bartlett's northern exploits.

Numerous small-town cafés dot the Baccalieu Trail, but none is more welcoming than **Country Corner** (14 Water St., 709/528-1099, May-Oct. daily 10am-6pm, lunches $5.50-9), where highlights include a bowl of steaming cod chowder and the blueberry crisp.

GETTING THERE

Brigus is 10 kilometers (10 minutes) north of Conception Harbour via Route 60 and about 85 kilometers (one hour) west of St. Johns via Route 1 and Route 70.

Hawthorne Cottage National Historic Site

Cupids

Plantation owner John Guy established Cuper's Cove in 1610, making what is now called Cupids the oldest British settlement in Canada. Artifacts can be seen at the worthwhile **Cupids Legacy Centre** (368 Seaforest Dr., 709/528-1610, www.cupidslegacycentre.ca, early June-early Oct. daily 9:30am-5pm, adult $8.50, senior $7.60, child $4.25), with many modern, interactive displays. Down on the waterfront and within walking distance of the Legacy Centre is the **Plantation Site,** an ongoing dig that continues to unearth the remains of Guy's plantation. Visitors are welcome to view the dig on 20-minute guided tours that leave on demand (book through Cupids Legacy Centre, early June-early Oct. daily 9am-5pm, adult $6, senior $4, child $3).

GETTING THERE

Cupids is about three kilometers north of Brigus via Keatings Road.

Harbour Grace

Once the second-largest town in Newfoundland, Harbour Grace suffered a series of setbacks when seven fires besieged the town over the span of a century. Many of its oldest buildings survived and now make up the **Harbour Grace Heritage District.** Named "Havre de Grace" by the French in the early 16th century, the town boasts both pirates and pilots in its heritage. **Conception Bay Museum** (Water St., 709/596-5465, July-Aug. daily 10am-5pm, adult $2, child $1) occupies the former site of the lair of Peter Easton, a notorious pirate of the early 1600s. It's in a three-story red-brick building along the harbor front. Three centuries later, on May 20, 1932, Harbour Grace gained fame when Amelia Earhart took off from the local airfield to become the first woman to fly solo across the Atlantic. The grassed runway of the Harbour Grace airfield is now a national historic site. To get there, follow Military Road from the main street through to the north side of town and take the signposted unpaved road under the highway to the top of the hill.

Before her famous flight, Amelia Earhart stayed at the red-brick **Hotel Harbour Grace** (66 Water St., 709/596-5156, www.hotelharbourgrace.ca, $90-120 s or d), but a better option today is the **Rothesay House Inn** (34 Water St., 709/596-2268 or 877/596-2268, www.rothesay.com, $140-160 s or d), where the four guest rooms have a distinct Victorian-era look. Rates include a cooked breakfast; dinner is $48 per person by advance reservation.

GETTING THERE

To get to Harbour Grace from Brigus, you can take Route 75 (32 kilometers, 30 minutes) or Route 70 (28 kilometers, 30 minutes) north. From St. John's, it's about 110 kilometers (1.5 hours) west and north along Route 1 and Route 70 to Harbour Grace.

Grates Cove

The peninsula's northernmost village, Grates Cove retains the look and feel of Ireland perhaps more than any other Irish-settled community, thanks to the hundreds of rock walls erected as livestock and farm enclosures by early settlers.

Off the eastern end of the peninsula's tip, the **Baccalieu Island Ecological Reserve** shelters 11 species of seabirds, including Leach's storm-petrels, black-legged kittiwakes, gannets, fulmars, and puffins.

GETTING THERE

To get to Grates Cove from Harbour Grace, it's a 75-kilometer (one hour) drive north on Route 70. From St. John's, it's about 180 kilometers (2.5 hours) to Grates Cove west along Route 1, then north on Route 75 and Route 70.

Heart's Content

The first successful transatlantic telegraph cables came ashore in 1866 at Heart's Content, 23 kilometers northwest of Carbonear. One of the original cables, which extended from Valentia Island on the west coast of Ireland, is still visible at the shoreline. Across the road, the restored **Heart's Content Cable**

Station (Rte. 80, 709/583-2160, mid-May-early Oct. daily 10:30am-5:30pm, adult $6, senior $4, child $3) displays some of the original equipment.

GETTING THERE

To get to Heart's Content from Grates Cove, take Route 70 south, then Route 80 south. It's a 60-kilometer (50-minute) drive. If you're driving directly to Heart's Content from St. John's, it's a 130-kilometer (1.5-hour) drive west along Route 1, then north along Route 75 and Route 74.

Dildo

Best known for its risqué name (thought to have been bestowed by Captain Cook in reference to a phallic offshore island), Dildo lies at the head of Trinity Bay, 12 kilometers north of the TransCanada Highway. The history of the 19th-century codfish hatchery on Dildo Island—the first commercial hatchery in Canada—is depicted at the **Dildo and Area Interpretation Centre** (Rte. 80, 709/582-2687, June-Sept. daily 10am-6pm, adult $2, child $1), along with a display of Dorset Inuit harpoon tips estimated to be 1,700 years old. Out front is a replica of an 8.5-meter-long squid pulled from local waters.

High above Trinity Bay, ★ **Inn by the Bay** (78 Front Rd., 709/582-3170 or 888/339-7829, www.dildoinns.com, $129-209 s or d) stacks up as equal to the best B&Bs in St. John's in all regards—with sweeping water views as a free extra. No stone has been left unturned in transforming this 1888 home into a six-room inn, right down to super-comfortable beds topped with feather-filled duvets and striking antiques that fill the veranda sunroom. Rates include a full breakfast and afternoon tea; dinner in the sea-level dining room, which overlooks the bay, is highly recommended.

GETTING THERE

To get to Dildo from Heart's Content, drive south on Route 80 for 45 kilometers (40 minutes). To get to Dildo directly from St. John's,

take Route 1 west, then Route 80 north, for a total of 100 kilometers (1.5 hours).

ST. JOHN'S TO FERRYLAND

From downtown St. John's, it's a little over 70 kilometers (one hour) to Ferryland, the ideal turnaround point for a day trip from the capital—except that there are a couple of stops en route worth as much time as you can afford.

★ Witless Bay Ecological Reserve

Newfoundland's seabird spectacle spreads across three offshore islands near the **Witless Bay Ecological Reserve,** 30 kilometers south of St. John's. Overwhelming displays of more than a million pairs of Atlantic puffins, Leach's storm-petrels, murres, black-legged kittiwakes, herring gulls, Atlantic razorbills, black guillemots, and black-backed and herring gulls are the attraction here. The season spans May-August and peaks mid-June-mid-July. Whale numbers in local waters have increased dramatically in the last two decades, and this is mirrored in the number of operators running whale-watching trips. Between May and September, you are most likely to see humpbacks, but killer, fin, and minke whales are also present throughout the reserve. Seeing icebergs is also a possibility.

The closest tour operators to St. John's are **O'Brien's Whale and Bird Tours** (Lower Rd., 709/753-4850 or 877/639-4253, adult $58, senior $53, child $30) and **Gatherall's Puffin and Whale Watch** (Northside Rd., 709/334-2887 or 800/419-4253), which are both based at Bay Bulls, 31 kilometers south. O'Brien's is a well-organized operation, complete with a choice of vessels and an onshore gift shop and restaurant. Pickups are available from any St. John's lodging (adult $25, child $20).

La Manche Provincial Park

La Manche Provincial Park was established in the 1960s to protect a scenic valley 53 kilometers south of St. John's along Route 10. The valley comes to an abrupt end at a cove surrounded by high cliffs, and here lies the most interesting aspect of the park. In 1840 a small village developed at the head of the cove, complete with a school, a general store, and wooden "flakes" for drying fish. In 1966 a wild winter storm destroyed most of the settlement. The government resettled the residents, and today concrete foundations and a reconstructed suspension bridge are all that remains. To get there, drive down the fire road beyond the park campground; from the gate, it's 1.5 kilometers to the cove (allow one hour for the round-trip). The **campground** (late May-late Sept., $18-28) has 69 campsites spread around two loops. There are no showers or hookups.

FERRYLAND

This east coast port, 70 kilometers south of St. John's, is one of Canada's oldest fishing villages, and the site of the colony founded by Sir George Calvert in 1621. To him, the region was akin to King Arthur's heavenly paradise, a haven for the beleaguered Roman Catholics from England. Or so he thought. Once settled at Ferryland, Calvert's colony endured diminishing supplies and harsh winters. His wife and son and a number of other colonists headed south to Maryland, and Calvert followed, leaving the plantation and the name of Avalon. Today, Ferryland is one of the most attractive communities on the Avalon Peninsula, but an archaeological dig in the heart of the community draws most visitors.

★ Colony of Avalon

An ongoing archaeological dig and a sparkling interpretive center combine to make the drive from St. John's worthwhile. The **Colony of Avalon Interpretation Centre** (709/432-3200, early June-Sept. daily 10am-6pm, adult $11.50, senior $10, student $9) is a big two-story building where display panels tell of Ferryland's long history, with the help of hundreds of artifacts used by the original settlers. Upstairs is a laboratory where you can watch archaeologists at work documenting the

finds. The herb garden out front replicates one from the era of the original Colony of Avalon.

From the interpretive center, it's a short walk through the modern-day village to the dig site, where you can watch archaeologists at work weekdays mid-June-mid-October. Admission to the interpretive center includes a 90-minute guided walk around the site, where you can see the remnants of a cobblestone street and the site of Calvert's mansion.

Shamrock Festival

The two-day **Shamrock Festival** (709/432-2052, www.ssfac.com) crowds the town on the last full weekend in July. Thousands of music fans gather within a roped-off area in the heart of the village (along with a few hundred on a distant hillside) to listen to some of Newfoundland's top musicians. The atmosphere is both welcoming and unforgettable—you'll find yourself surrounded by the lilt of Irish accents, the smells of an outdoor fair mixed with fresh ocean air, and the sounds of foot-stomping Celtic music. A plastic cup of Quidi Vidi beer rounds out the experience.

Food

Ferryland doesn't have a great deal of visitor services, but as most visitors are day-trippers from the capital, this isn't a problem.

Earn your lunch by walking up to the headland, through town, to reach ★ **Lighthouse Picnics** (709/363-7456, mid-June-mid-Sept. Wed.-Sun. 11:30am-4:30pm, adult $26, child $13), which operates out of the red-and-white 1870 lighthouse. Each picnic consists of a sandwich, salad, a dessert, and freshly squeezed lemonade, with options such as crab cakes and baked-daily muffins. Picnic baskets—along with blankets—are supplied. Reservations in summer are a must, so call ahead or visit www.lighthousepicnics.ca for a link to their email.

Getting There

Ferryland is about 70 kilometers (one hour) south of St. John's via Route 10.

CONTINUING ALONG THE IRISH LOOP

From Ferryland, Route 10 continues south for 58 kilometers, then heads west and north as Route 90 to St. Catherines. From this point, you can head south to Cape St. Mary's or north past Salmonier Nature Park back to the TransCanada Highway. This comprises the Irish Loop. While almost 50 percent of Newfoundlanders are of Irish descent, the strong accents and Celtic traditions are more prevalent here than elsewhere in the province.

Mistaken Point Ecological Reserve

At the southern end of the Avalon Peninsula, **Mistaken Point Ecological Reserve** lies alongside a remote coastline. To explore the area, turn off Route 10 at Portugal Cove South and follow the unmarked gravel road 16 kilometers to Long Beach, where the reserve's gently rolling headland stretches to the sea. Bring a warm jacket to fend off the strong winds, and be ready for thick fog banks June-mid-July. Hikers enjoy the trails that meander across the reserve, and photographers relish the offshore boulders and turbulent surf. The rocks at the ecological reserve, acclaimed as

one of Canada's most important fossil sites, contain impressions of 20 different species of multicellular marine creatures that lived 620 million years ago.

Salmonier Nature Park

Salmonier Nature Park, on Route 90 halfway between the TransCanada Highway and St. Catherines (709/229-7189, June-Aug. daily 10am-5pm, Sept. daily 10am-3pm, free) is well worth searching out. A two-kilometer boardwalk and wood-chip trail runs through a sample forest and across bogs, which back up to the Avalon Wilderness Reserve. Moose, caribou, lynx, bald eagles, snowy owls, otters, beavers, mink, and other indigenous species are exhibited in natural-habitat enclosures.

CAPE SHORE

The Cape Shore juts into Placentia Bay west of the main body of the Avalon Peninsula. It's 215 kilometers from the TransCanada Highway, south through Salmonier to St. Bride's, and back to the TransCanada Highway, 33 kilometers west of the starting point. The highlight of the region is the bird colony at Cape St. Mary's.

A whale greets one of O'Brien's Whale and Bird Tours.

Argentia

Argentia operated as a U.S. naval base between 1941 and 1994, with up to 20,000 American servicemen stationed there during World War II. Ferries operate out of one of the original ports, but most buildings have been demolished. The entire site is wide open and there are few restrictions to wandering around, with unofficial trails leading to lookouts, abandoned bunkers, and good vantage points for watching seabirds.

Beyond the ferry terminal is **Argentia Provincial Visitor Information Centre** (709/227-5272), which opens in conjunction with ferry arrivals. From Argentia, drive south through Placentia to reach Cape St. Mary's or head northwest along Route 100 to the TransCanada Highway, which leads into downtown St. John's.

GETTING THERE

Argentia is 8 kilometers north of Placentia (via Charter Avenue) and 130 kilometers (1.5 hours) southwest of St. John's via the TransCanada Highway and Route 100.

One of two ferry services to Newfoundland from North Sydney (Nova Scotia) docks at Argentia. Ferries are operated by **Marine Atlantic** (709/227-2431 or 800/341-7981, www.marine-atlantic.ca, adult $125, senior $115, child $62, from $253 for vehicles) two times weekly mid-June-late September (at other times of year, you will need to use the Sydney to Port-aux-Basques route). The trip over from the mainland takes 14 hours; dorm beds and cabins are available.

Placentia

France chose the magnificent coastal forest area overlooking Placentia Bay for its early island capital, Plaisance, and colonists and soldiers settled here in 1662. The early military fortification crowned a high hill overlooking the port at what is now Jerseyside. The French launched assaults on St. John's from Le Gaillardin, the first small fort of 1692, and then from Fort Royal, the massive stone fortress built the following year. England gained possession of the settlement in 1713 and renamed it Placentia. The hill on which the fortress stands became known as Castle Hill. Exhibits at the visitors center of **Castle Hill National Historic Site** (709/227-2401, June-Aug. daily 10am-6pm, adult $4, senior $3.50, child $2) document French and English history at Placentia. Guided tours are offered in summer. Picnic tables are available, and trails

a guided tour through the Colony of Avalon

run along the peak's fortifications and the bay's stone beach.

GETTING THERE

Placentia is 130 kilometers southwest of St. John's, 8 kilometers south of Argentia via Charter Avenue. Get there via the TransCanada Highway and Route 100.

★ Cape St. Mary's Ecological Reserve

The **Cape St. Mary's Ecological Reserve** lies at the Cape Shore's southern tip, 16 kilometers down an unpaved road off Route 100. If you're traveling down from St. John's, allow at least 2.5 hours; from the ferry terminal at Argentia, head south for 73 kilometers (allow at least an hour). At the end of the road is an **interpretive center** (709/277-1666, mid-May-early Oct. daily 9am-5pm, free). From this point, a one-kilometer trail leads across the steeply banked headland to North America's most accessible bird sanctuary. You'll hear the birds long before they come into view. And then all of a sudden, Bird Rock emerges in front of you—a 60-meter-high sea stack jammed with some 60,000 seabirds. The rocky pyramid seems to come alive with fluttering, soaring birds, whose noisy calls drift out to sea on the breezes. Expect to see northern gannets in one of North America's largest colonies (10,000 nesting pairs), common and thick-billed murres, and black-legged kittiwakes, along with some razorbills, black guillemots, great black-backed gulls, and herring gulls.

Warning: The trail is often slippery and comes very close to precipitous cliffs, so be very careful. Also, be prepared for bad weather by dressing warmly and in layers.

The closest accommodation to Cape St. Mary's is **Bird Island Resort** (64 Main Rd., 709/337-2450, www.birdislandresort.com, $85-130 s or d), in St. Bride's, 20 kilometers north. Overlooking Placentia Bay, the "resort" comprises five motel rooms, 15 kitchen-equipped cottages, lawn games, a convenience store, and a launderette.

GETTING THERE

The reserve is 73 kilometers (one hour) south of Argentia via Route 100. It's 170 kilometers (2.5 hours) southwest of St. John's via Route 1, Route 90, and Route 92.

Cape St. Mary's Ecological Reserve

Central and Western Newfoundland

Burin Peninsula and Vicinity 46

Bonavista Peninsula 49

Clarenville to Deer Lake.............. 53

Deer Lake to Port-aux-Basques....... 59

Gros Morne National Park............ 66

Visualize the island of Newfoundland as not one island but two, similarly shaped but different in size—a mammoth main island and a smaller one. This chapter covers the former—everything west of the Avalon Peninsula.

The "two islands" are linked by an isthmus that begins an hour's drive west from St. John's. Beyond the turnoff to the delightfully named village of Come by Chance, the TransCanada Highway enters the meaty part of the island. Think of this highway as a long Main Street. The horseshoe-shaped route edges the interior and connects the Avalon Peninsula with Channel-Port-aux-Basques—a 905-kilometer journey. Well-marked side roads split off the main highway and whisk drivers onto the peninsulas. Aside from the Burin Peninsula's efficient Route 210 and the Northern Peninsula's relatively uncomplicated Route 430, the other side roads to the peninsulas and coastlines meander interminably.

The appeal of raw wilderness aside, this vast part of Newfoundland caters to numerous interests. Majestic icebergs wander into fjords and coves on the northern coastlines. All along the seacoasts, photogenic lighthouses perch atop precipitous cliffs overlooking the surf. Sightseers line up for boat tours led by knowledgeable skippers or academically trained guides, whose vessels nose among whales, seals, and icebergs. If you're interested in a quick trip to France, you can visit a remnant of the long-ago age of exploration: Fortune on the Burin Peninsula is just a two-hour boat ride from St-Pierre, the capital of France's archipelago province of St-Pierre and Miquelon. The ancient world heaved and formed richly diverse landscapes at Gros Morne National Park. A millennium ago, the Vikings arrived and established a coastal camp (North America's first European settlement), now re-created at L'Anse aux Meadows National Historic Site.

PLANNING YOUR TIME

While the previous chapter covered a small corner of the province, in this chapter, distances will prove to be important when

---

Previous: Lobster Cove Head Lighthouse; lobster pots. **Above:** moose and caribou carvings.

Look for ★ to find recommended sights, activities, dining, and lodging.

Highlights

★ **Trinity:** Step back in time at this quintessential Newfoundland village with brightly painted, saltbox-style houses lining its narrow lanes (page 49).

★ **Iceberg-Viewing:** You can see icebergs from various points along the northern Newfoundland coast, but one of the most reliable spots is Twillingate (page 56).

★ **Tablelands:** You'll be lost for words scrambling through its moonlike terrain (page 69).

★ **Boat Tours in Gros Morne National Park:** Take to Western Brook Pond for neck-straining views of an ancient, glacially carved fjord (page 70).

★ **Thrombolites of Flowers Cove:** Never heard of thrombolites? Most people haven't. But don't blink—even though these rare fossils occur in only two places on Earth, they're not signposted as you drive north along the Viking Trail (page 78).

★ **L'Anse aux Meadows:** Follow in the footsteps of the Vikings by exploring the tip of the Northern Peninsula (page 80).

★ **Burnt Cape Ecological Reserve:** This remote limestone outcrop is home to more rare and endangered species of plants than anywhere else in Atlantic Canada (page 82).

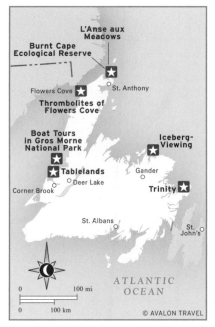

Central and Western Newfoundland

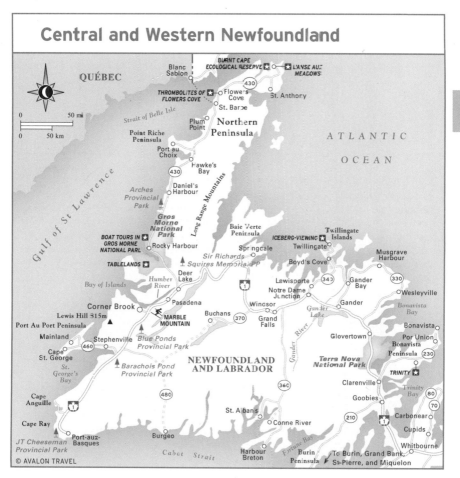

© AVALON TRAVEL

planning how and where to spend your time. For example, from St. John's, it's 640 kilometers to Deer Lake, 905 kilometers to the ferry terminal at Port-aux-Basques, and almost 1,100 kilometers to St. Anthony at the tip of the Northern Peninsula.

The time you spend in the central and western regions of Newfoundland obviously ties in with your travels to St. John's and the Avalon Peninsula. Traveling to the Bonavista Peninsula and villages like **Trinity** can be a two-day trip from the capital, but travel any farther west and you're committed to driving clear across the island. If you're catching the ferry from Port-aux-Basques, allow at least

five days to get there from the capital. This would allow a night at Trinity, a detour from the TransCanada Highway to go **iceberg-viewing** at Twillingate, and a couple of days exploring **Gros Morne National Park,** where highlights include hiking through the **Tablelands** and taking a boat tour on **Western Brook Pond.**

What this five-day suggestion doesn't take into consideration is the **Northern Peninsula,** which is one of my favorite places in all of Canada. Its 470 amazing kilometers stretch from Deer Lake to the tip of the peninsula. With time spent exploring the region's beautiful coastline, as well as stops at the thrombolites of Flowers Cove, L'Anse aux Meadows, and Burnt Cape Ecological Reserve, add at least four days to your cross-province schedule from St. John's to Port-aux-Basques. If you're returning a rental vehicle to St. John's, give the stretch of highway south of Deer Lake a miss, but still add two days to the total trip. By flying in and out of Deer Lake, you can concentrate your time in Gros Morne National Park and the Northern Peninsula—an ideal scenario for outdoors lovers.

Burin Peninsula and Vicinity

The 200-kilometer-long Burin Peninsula angles like a kicking boot off Newfoundland's southeastern coastline. The peninsula's interior is a primeval, barren moonscape—if the moon had water, that is, for every hollow and depression in these barrens is filled with bogs, marshes, and ponds. But the coastline rims the edge of the Grand Banks, historically one of the most fertile fishing regions in North America. Along the shore are scattered fishing villages and several burgeoning towns. Marystown, one of the fastest-growing towns in the province, is supported by one of the largest fish-processing plants in eastern Canada, and its shipyard supplies vessels to the booming North Atlantic oil industry. St. Lawrence is the exception to the region; as Canada's only producer of the mineral fluorite, it has relied on mining as much as on marine-related industries. For the most part, however, fishing has been the mainstay of the peninsula's communities since the 1500s.

BOAT HARBOUR

A cottage industry here produces hand-hooked scenic mats made of reused fabric scraps. The mats and other homemade wares are sold at reasonable prices at the Tea Rose (Rte. 210, 709/443-2580, summer daily noon-7pm), about one kilometer south of the Boat Harbour intersection, where you can also get light meals.

Getting There

Boat Harbour is 270 kilometers (3.5 hours) west of St. John's via the TransCanada Highway and Route 210.

BURIN

Near the "heel" of the boot-shaped peninsula, Burin, settled in the early 1700s, lies in the lee of offshore islands. The islands generally protect the town from the open Atlantic, though they weren't enough to stop a destructive tidal wave in 1929. The islands also were a refuge for pirates, who could escape their pursuers among the dangerous channels. During his mapping expeditions of the Newfoundland coast in the 1760s, Captain James Cook used Burin as a seasonal headquarters. A high hill above the town, where watch was kept for smugglers and illegal fishing, still bears his name—Cook's Lookout.

Over the second weekend of July, the Festival of Folk Song and Dance (709/891-2655, day pass $8 pp) is a three-day extravaganza of Irish-inspired music making, children's games, seafood meals, and craft shows and sales. The festival ranks among Newfoundland's most popular heritage events.

A comfortable, no-frills accommodation is the Burin Peninsula Motel (33 Grandview Blvd., 709/832-2180, $99-109 s or d). The 10 guest rooms are basic and come with small TVs, but do have wireless Internet.

Getting There

Burin is about 60 kilometers (one hour) south of Boat Harbour via Route 210. It's about 310 kilometers (4-4.5 hours) southwest of St. John's via Route 1 and Route 210.

GRAND BANK

Grand Bank, on the "toe" of the Burin boot, is the best known of the peninsula's towns. Settled in the 1650s by the French and taken over by the British in the early 1700s, Grand Bank (pop. 2,500) has always been associated with the rich fishing grounds of the same name, the Grand Banks to the south and west of Newfoundland.

The **Heritage Walk** visits the province's largest number of Queen Anne-style homes outside of St. John's. The historic district's architectural treasures include the 1905 **Masonic Lodge,** the 1917 **Thorndyke House** (with its Masonic symbolism integrated into the interior design), and the **George C. Harris House** (16 Water St., 709/832-1574, July-Aug. daily 10am-4pm, adult $3). The latter is a 1908 Queen Anne building housing the town's museum. Complementing the Heritage Walk are the Nature Trail, leading to a lookout and salmon spawning beds, and the Marine Trail, which closely follows the shoreline of Fortune Bay to the **Mariners' Memorial.**

After extensive renovations in 2011, the **Provincial Seamen's Museum** (54 Marine Dr., 709/832-1484, May-Sept. Mon.-Sat. 9am-4:30pm, Sun. noon-4:30pm, adult $2.50) is difficult to miss. Styled as an angular white sailing ship, the museum has exhibits on the Grand Banks fisheries and maritime history, with photographs, ship models, and other artifacts.

Getting There

Grand Bank is almost 60 kilometers (one hour) west of Burin via Routes 210 and 222. It's 360 kilometers (4.5 hours) southwest of St. John's via Route 1 and Route 210.

ST-PIERRE AND MIQUELON

Centuries of fierce British and French battles ended in the mid-1700s with Britain's dominance firmly stamped across eastern Canada—*except* on St-Pierre and Miquelon, a trio of islands 25 kilometers south of the Newfoundland mainland. Today, this geopolitical oddity is not part of Atlantic Canada, but rather a *département* of France and the last toehold of France's once-vast holdings in North America.

St-Pierre and Miquelon are French in all regards. Unlike traveling to French regions of Canada, there is a lot more than a foreign language to deal with. Canadians must show photo identification, such as a driver's license or passport. Entry for all other nationalities mirrors entry requirements for France; in other words, a passport is required for U.S. citizens.

Legal tender is the euro (€), but some (not all) businesses accept U.S. and Canadian dollars at fair bank rates. Electrical current throughout St-Pierre and Miquelon is 220 volts, although the bigger hotels have converters.

The islands even have their own time zone—30 minutes ahead of Newfoundland time.

Sights

St-Pierre and Miquelon consists of three islands, with a combined land area of about 242 square kilometers. Tiny **St-Pierre** is the name of the smallest island, as well as a bustling town (pop. 6,300). The topography of this triangular island includes hills, bogs, and ponds in the north, and lowlands in the south. The larger islands are **Miquelon,** which is home to a village of the same name (pop. 600), and uninhabited **Petite Miquelon** (also called Langlade). These two islands are joined by a sand-dune isthmus.

The capital, St-Pierre is the most popular destination. It dates to the early 1600s, when French fishermen, mainly from Brittany, worked offshore. The port's mood and appearance are pervasively French, with bistros, cafés, bars, brasseries, wrought-iron balconies, and an abundance of Gallic pride. St-Pierre borders a sheltered harbor filled with colorful fishing boats and backed by narrow lanes that radiate uphill from the harbor. The cemetery, two blocks inland from rue du 11 Novembre, has an interesting arrangement of aboveground graves, similar to those in New Orleans.

One of the islands' greatest attractions, of course, is the low duty rates on French wines and other goods. Visitors may bring back $200 worth of duty-free purchases after a 48-hour visit. You'll find shops with French wines, perfumes, and jewelry.

Food

Make your way through the streets of St-Pierre and it's difficult not to be tempted by the sweet smells coming from the many patisseries and cafés. A favorite is **Les Delices de Josephine** (508/41-20-27, Mon.-Sat. 11:30am-6pm, lunches €6.50-11), which has delicious coffee, a great selection of teas, pastries made daily from scratch, and a selection of hot lunch items such as quiche.

One of the best choices for a casual meal is **Le Feu de Braise** (14 rue Albert Briand, 508/41-91-60, daily noon-2:30pm and 6pm-10pm, €15-21), a bright room offering a menu dominated by classic French bistro-style dishes.

Accommodations

Because the number of guest rooms is limited, make all lodging arrangements before arriving.

For its beautiful rooms and friendly atmosphere, my favorite island accommodation is **Auberge Saint-Pierre** (16 rue Georges Daguerre, 508/41-40-86, www.aubergesaintpierre.fr, from €131 s or d). A breakfast of hot and cold French specialties is an additional €10.50 per person.

Among the dozen small hotels, pensions, and B&Bs, the largest lodging is the 43-room **Hôtel Robert** (2 rue du 11 Novembre, 508/41-24-19, www.hotelrobert.com, €90-150 s or d), along the harbor front (only the most expensive rooms have water views) and within walking distance of the ferry wharf. Having hosted the American gangster Al Capone in the 1920s, this three-story lodging itself oozes historic charm, yet the renovated rooms have contemporary furnishings.

Information

Once on the island, the best source of information is the **St-Pierre & Miquelon Tourist Office** (rue Antoine Soucy, 508/41-02-00, www.tourisme-saint-pierre-et-miquelon. com). The website has links to island accommodations as well as tour bundles that include accommodations.

Getting There

Air Saint Pierre (902/873-3566, www.airsaintpierre.com) flies year-round between St-Pierre and St. John's for $350-415 round-trip. The airline also flies into St-Pierre from Halifax, Sydney (Nova Scotia), and Montréal.

Le Cabestan (709/832-3455 or 855/832-3455; www.saintpierreferry.ca, round-trip adult $93, senior $88, child $58) is a high-speed passenger ferry that operates between Fortune, on the Burin Peninsula, and St-Pierre once daily July-August and four days a week April-June and September.

Bonavista Peninsula

The Bonavista Peninsula rises off the eastern coastline as a broad, bent finger covered with verdant woods, farmlands, and rolling hills. Paved Route 230 runs along the peninsula's length, from the TransCanada Highway to the town of Bonavista at the tip; Route 235 returns to Highway 1 along the peninsula's west side.

CLARENVILLE

Founded in 1890, Clarenville, along the TransCanada Highway, 190 kilometers from St. John's, serves as the gateway to the Bonavista Peninsula. The town of 6,000 is relatively new compared to the rest of Newfoundland and offers few reasons to stop other than to rest your head for the night.

Along the TransCanada Highway are two larger motels. From St. John's, the first of these is the **Clarenville Inn** (134 TransCanada Hwy., 709/466-7911 or 877/466-7911, www.clarenvilleinn.ca, from $120 s or d), which fronts the highway, offering 63 rooms with wireless Internet and an outdoor heated pool. One of the best things about this lodging is **Stellar Kitchen,** a restaurant with sweeping views across the town and bay (daily for breakfast, lunch, and dinner, $15-25). In town itself, the **Restland Motel** (Memorial Dr., 709/466-7636, www.restlandmotel.ca, from $95 s or d) has a mix of 24 midsize air-conditioned motel rooms and kitchen-equipped units. On-site is a restaurant and pub, and across the road is a shopping mall.

Getting There

Clarenville is 190 kilometers (two hours) northwest of St. John's via Route 1.

★ TRINITY

Just three years after John Cabot bumped into Newfoundland, Portugal commissioned mariners Gaspar and Miguel Côrte-Real to search for a passage to China. That mission failed, but Gaspar accidentally sailed into Trinity Bay on Trinity Sunday in 1501. In 1558, merchants from England's West Country founded a settlement on the same site, making it even older than St. Augustine, Florida.

The attractive village of Trinity (pop. 400) has changed little since the late 1800s. White

Many of Trinity's historic buildings are open to the public.

picket fences, small gardens, and historic homes are everywhere. The best photo vantage point of Trinity is from the Route 239 coastal spur, the narrow road also known as Courthouse Road. The road peels across the headlands, turns a quick corner, and suddenly overlooks the seaport. Ease into the turn so you can savor the view. (To get a photograph, park your car in the village and walk back up the road.) Once down in the village proper, park your car and explore on foot.

Sights

The **Trinity Visitor Centre** (Rte. 239, 709/729-0592, mid-May-mid-Oct. daily 9:30am-5pm), in a handsomely restored building, has historical exhibits about the village. **Mercantile Premises** (West St., 709/464-2042, mid-May-mid-Oct. daily 9:30am-5pm) is a restored 1820s general store. In the 1800s, Emma Hiscock and her two daughters lived in the restored mustard-and-green **Hiscock House** (Church Rd., mid-May-mid-Oct. daily 9:30am-5pm), a block inland from the government wharf. They operated a forge, retail store, and telegraph office in the saltbox-style house. These three attractions are operated by the province; combined admission is adult $6, child $3.

The following buildings, scattered through the village, are looked after by the **Trinity Historical Society** (709/464-3599, www.trinityhistoricalsociety.com, mid-May-mid-Oct. daily 9:30am-5pm, $20 for all four buildings plus the three detailed above, children free). **Lester Garland House** is an imposing Georgian-style red-brick mansion that has been restored to its 1820s appearance and now houses a museum. The **Green Family Forge** (Church Rd.), in a restored 1895 building, is a blacksmith museum displaying more than 1,500 tools, products, and other artifacts of the blacksmith trade. Also on Church Road is an 1880 saltbox-style house that now serves as the **Trinity Society Museum,** displaying more than 2,000 fishing, mercantile, medical, and firefighting artifacts. Although there has been a cooperage (barrel maker) in Trinity since the 1700s, **The Cooperage** is a modern replica of what a similar business would have looked like in times gone by. In summer, you can watch coopers here creating barrels and other wooden objects using traditional techniques.

Entertainment and Events

The summer solstice kicks off Rising Tide Theatre's **Summer in the Bight**

a performance by Summer in the Bight

(709/464-3232, www.risingtidetheatre.com), presenting original musical and dramatic productions written and performed by some of Newfoundland's best writers and actors. The theater is a re-created fishing shed on Green's Point, at the eastern side of the village. Performances are scheduled 2-3 times a week and cost $28.50 ($43.50 for the dinner theater).

Accommodations

Right on the water, the ★ Artisan Inn (57 High St., 709/464-3377 or 877/464-7700, www.trinityvacations.com, May-mid-Oct., $140-210 s or d) is set up as a retreat for artists—if views from the oceanfront studio don't inspire you, nothing will—but everyone is welcome. It offers two en suite rooms and a kitchen-equipped suite. The adjacent Campbell House holds an additional three guest rooms. Rates include breakfast, and dinner is available at the in-house Twine Loft with advance notice, with set menus offered at 5:30pm and 7:45pm seatings.

Getting There

Trinity is 70 kilometers (one hour) northeast of Clarenville along Route 230. From St. John's, Trinity is 270 kilometers (3.5 hours) west on Route 1 and north on Route 230.

PORT UNION

The only town in Canada to have been established by a labor union, Port Union lies 32 kilometers past Trinity. The oldest part of town is across the bay from the fish-processing plant. Turn right as you enter the village and you'll soon find yourself in Port Union South, passing through a narrow street of boarded-up company warehouses. Beyond these is Port Union Historical Museum (Main St., 709/469-2728, mid-June-Aug. daily 11am-5pm, adult $2, child $1), housed in a waterfront 1917 railway station. Once you've read up on the town's history, backtrack and take a left turn through a narrow rock cleft to Bungalow Hill for sweeping harbor views.

Getting There

From Trinity, it's 30 kilometers (30 minutes) northeast on Route 230 to Port Union. To get to Port Union from St. John's, take Highway 1 west and Route 230 north for a total of 290 kilometers (four hours).

looking down to the Artisan Inn

BONAVISTA

Fifty kilometers up Route 230 from Trinity, Bonavista (pop. 5,000) is a surprisingly large town that sprawls across the far reaches of the Bonavista Peninsula. The town began in the 1600s as a French fishing port, but many believe **Cape Bonavista,** six kilometers north of town, was the first landfall of Giovanni Caboto (better known as John Cabot), who visited the region in 1497.

Sights

Downtown Bonavista centers on a harbor filled with fishing boats and surrounded by a colorful array of homes and businesses. The historic highlight is **Ryan Premises** (corner of Ryan's Hill and Old Catalina Rd., 709/468-1600, June-Aug. daily 10am-6pm, adult $4, senior $3.50, child $2), where merchant James Ryan established his salt-fish enterprise in the mid-1800s. The site's collection of white clapboard buildings includes a fish store and a re-created retail shop. Across the road is the original manager's residence. All buildings are filled with exhibits and artifacts of the era. In the salt shed, local crafters demonstrate such skills as furniture making; their goods can be purchased in the retail shop.

Also worth searching out downtown is **The Elephant Shop** (8 Ackerman's Ln., 709/468-8145, May-Oct. Tues.-Sun. 11am-5pm), a wooden residence dating to the late 1800s that has been transformed into a boutique selling high-quality clothing and jewelry, which is well worth visiting for both the history and shopping experience. The spacious attic of the home has been transformed into **The Aleksandrs International Gallery of Fine Art** (same contact information and hours), with a high ceiling, funky wall angles, and a contemporary do-over creating a unique space where original art from varied destinations such as the High Arctic and Australia is displayed.

Signposted through town, the 1871 **Mockbeggar Plantation** (Mockbeggar Rd., 709/468-7300, mid-May-mid-Oct. daily 9:30am-5pm, adult $6, senior $4, child $3) is a whitewashed waterfront building surrounded by a white picket fence. It has been a residence, carpenter's shop, and fish store.

Beyond Mockbeggar Plantation, the photogenic 1843 **Cape Bonavista Lighthouse** (Rte. 230, 709/468-7444, mid-May-early-Oct. daily 9:30am-5pm, adult $6, senior $4, child $3) crowns a steep and rocky headland. The keeper's quarters inside the red-and-white-striped tower have been restored to the 1870 period. A climb up steep steps leads to the original catoptric light with Argand oil burners and reflectors.

Accommodations

Bonavista makes a pleasant day trip from Trinity, but if you want to stay longer, there are numerous options. The most luxurious by far, and one of the finest accommodations in all of Newfoundland, is ★ **Elizabeth J. Cottages** (Harris St., 709/468-8145, www.elizabethjcottages.com, May-Oct., $325 s or d). The cottages enjoy an absolute oceanfront setting on the edge of town; their design was inspired by the old saltbox homes still common throughout the region, but beyond the layout, no expense has been spared in creating a luxurious environment in which to soak up the sweeping ocean views. The two-bedroom units are awash in natural light and feature niceties such as freshly baked bread upon arrival, 650-thread-count sheets, and plush bathrobes. Other features include private decks with slick outdoor furniture and barbecues, modem hookups, TV/DVD combos, and laundry facilities.

If your tastes are a little simpler, the four **Oceanside Cabins** (195 Cape Shore Rd., 709/468-7771, $125-145 s or d), with basic kitchens and Wi-Fi, should suffice.

Getting There

Allow 20 minutes to reach Bonavista from Port Union, which is 20 kilometers south via Route 230. To get to Bonavista from St. John's, take Highway 1 west and Route 230 north for a total of 310 kilometers (just over four hours).

Clarenville to Deer Lake

It's 450 kilometers from Clarenville to Deer Lake. The TransCanada Highway linking these two towns cuts across the interior in a rambling inland path, sometimes angling north to touch a deeply carved bay or reaching into the interior to amble amid the plateau's seemingly endless stretches of tree-blanketed hills. The best chance to get up close and personal with this region is at Terra Nova National Park, but there are also many worthwhile detours, such as to Twillingate, famous for its iceberg-watching tours.

TERRA NOVA NATIONAL PARK

The TransCanada Highway enters **Terra Nova National Park** 35 kilometers north of Clarenville, and for the next 50 kilometers it travels within the park boundary. But to really see the park, divert from the highway to remote bodies of fish-filled freshwater, through forests inhabited by moose and bears, and to the rugged coastline where kayakers glide through protected waters and bald eagles soar overhead.

Park Entry

You don't need a pass to drive through the national park, but if you plan on stopping for any reason, you must pay admission (adult $6, senior $5, child $3). Your payment is valid until 4pm the following day.

Park Visitor Centre

Make your first stop the **Park Visitor Centre** (709/533-2942, mid-May-June and Sept.-early-Oct. Thurs.-Mon. 10am-4pm, July-Aug. daily 10am-6pm, free with park admission). Overlooking Newman Sound at Salton's Brook, it is one kilometer off the TransCanada Highway, 35 kilometers north of where it first enters the park. The center features small aquariums, touch tanks, a live feed from an underwater camera, exhibits on the various marine habitats within the park, interactive computer displays, and films, plus a restaurant and gift shop. The center's gift shop sells topographical maps of the park and stocks books about the province's flora, fauna, and attractions.

Hiking

More than a dozen trails thread through the park, providing some 60 kilometers of hiking. Most are uncomplicated loop routes that meander easily for an hour's walk beneath tree canopies. From the Park Visitor Centre, the one-kilometer **Heritage Trail** leads along Salton's Brook, and a three-kilometer (one-way) trail leads to picturesque and quiet **Blue Hill Pond.** Another three-kilometer trail follows the edge of **Sandy Pond,** starting from 13 kilometers south of the Park Visitor Centre. The longest trek, the 55-kilometer **Outport Trail,** requires backcountry camping skills. Most hikers spend one or two nights on the trail, which is notable for the opportunities it affords to see icebergs and whales.

Water Sports

Take a break from the saltwater by planning to spend time at **Sandy Pond,** a shallow body of water 13 kilometers south of the Park Visitor Centre and 12 kilometers north of the southern park boundary This day-use area has canoe and kayak rentals (709/677-2221, $10 for 30 minutes), allows swimming, and is encircled by a three-kilometer walking trail (allow one hour).

Food and Accommodations

While there are no accommodations within park boundaries, the following two options lie on the edge of the park.

The village of Charlottetown occupies a pocket of oceanfront land 15 kilometers north of the park, outside the official park boundary. Here you'll find the trim **Clode**

Sound Motel (709/664-3146, www.clodesound.com, May-Oct., $120-150 s or d). It has 18 rooms and a three-bedroom cottage ($210), an outdoor swimming pool, a playground, a tennis court, a wood-fired barbecue, and wireless Internet. Also on the premises is a highly regarded restaurant (summer daily 8am-10pm) that serves wonderful desserts created with apples from the motel's 90-year-old orchard.

Just beyond the south end of the park is **Terra Nova Resort** (TransCanada Hwy., 709/543-2525, www.terranovagolf.com, May-Oct., from $165 s or d), a full-service resort built alongside the Twin Rivers Golf Course, where golfers get to walk some of Canada's finest fairways for the bargain price of $60 midweek and $69 on weekends. Other amenities include tennis courts, an outdoor heated pool, hiking trails, the **Clode Sound Dining Room** (May-Oct. daily for breakfast, lunch, and dinner, $27-36), and a pub. The 83 guest rooms feature solid furnishings and a contemporary feel. Children are catered to with a schedule of activities that includes treasure hunts, craft sessions, and picnic lunches.

Camping

Wooded **Newman Sound Campground** (tents $28, hookups $32) has 387 full- and semi-serviced campsites, kitchen shelters, heated washrooms with hot showers, a Nature House (June-Sept. daily 10am-5pm), a launderette, and a daily interpretive program. Reservations are taken for 40 percent of the sites through **Parks Canada** (877/737-3783, www.pccamping.ca). The cost is $11 per reservation, plus the camping fee. The campground turnoff is 30 kilometers north of the southern park boundary. A 4.5-kilometer trail along Newman Sound links the campground with the Park Visitor Centre.

From the park's northern edge, head five kilometers east on Route 310 to reach **Malady Head Campground** ($22.50 per site). The facility has a kitchen/activity area and a playground.

Getting There

The entrance to Terra Nova National Park is 70 kilometers (40 minutes) north of Clarenville via Highway 1. To get to the park from St. John's, take Highway 1 west and north for 250 kilometers (three hours).

GANDER

The town of Gander (population 11,000) is halfway between Newfoundland's two largest cities (350 kilometers from St. John's and 357 kilometers from Corner Brook). It was founded in 1951, when the military decided to convert Gander Airport to civilian operations, and so it's fitting that the main attractions today revolve around air travel.

Gateway to North America

When aircraft cross the Atlantic Ocean from Europe, they enter North American airspace somewhere off the coast of Newfoundland. In the early days of aviation, this meant that the planes needed somewhere to refuel, and so Gander grew as a stopping point for all types of aviation. Although commercial transatlantic flights no longer need to refuel at Gander, the airport retains its importance, such as after the terrorist attacks of September 11, 2001, when 39 commercial planes carrying more than 6,500 crew and passengers were diverted to Gander. Even if you're not departing on one of the scheduled Air Canada or Provincial Airlines flights, it's worth dropping by **Gander International Airport,** on the northeastern side of downtown, to view the many displays and memorabilia through the main terminal.

Gleaming full-size models of World War II Hudson, Voodoo, and Canso water bombers, a Beech 18 aircraft, and a reconstructed De Havilland Tiger Moth greet visitors to the **North Atlantic Aviation Museum** (135 TransCanada Hwy., 709/256-2923, summer daily 9am-7pm, the rest of the year Mon.-Fri. 9am-5pm, adult $6, senior and child $5). Inside, exhibits on Gander's strategic role in World War II and the development of transatlantic aviation include early equipment,

Gander

To Twillingate

MCCURDY DR

GANDER BAY RD

MEMORIAL DR

FITZMAURICE

BOYD

GRANDY AVE

COTTON ST

To Deer
Lake

MACDONALD DR

BOWLES ST

LINDBERGH

AIRPORT BLVD

To
Airport

HAMILTON

EARHART

BISHOP

RD

FRASER

BROCHEN

HAWKER CRESCENT

JUNGLE
JIM'S

ST. ELIZABETH

SULLIVAN

NORTH ATLANTIC
AVIATION MUSEUM

COMFORT
INN

0   500 yds

0   500 m

HOTEL GANDER

DR

Gander
Lake

To Silent Witness
Memorial and St. John's

© AVALON TRAVEL

uniforms, photographs, and a reconstructed DC-3 cockpit.

The **Silent Witness Memorial,** four kilometers east of town and one kilometer south along an unpaved road, marks the site of an aviation disaster. On a cold December day in 1985, the airport was a scheduled refueling stop for a DC-8 flight from the Middle East. The flight carried the U.S. 101st Airborne Division, better known as the Screaming Eagles, who were returning home from a United Nations peacekeeping mission in the Sinai. The plane, with 248 soldiers and an eight-member crew, crashed shortly after takeoff between the highway and Gander Lake, killing all onboard. A group of statues, of an American soldier and two children, backed by Canadian, U.S., and Newfoundland flags, overlooks the lake. The memorial spreads across the rocky hillside, and flower bouquets lie here and there.

Food and Accommodations

Gander is a convenient stop for travelers crossing Newfoundland's interior, and it provides a wide choice of accommodations. The two-story **Comfort Inn** (112 TransCanada Hwy., 709/256-3535, www.choicehotels.ca, $115 s, $125 d, including a continental breakfast buffet) has 64 spacious and relatively modern guest rooms. Facilities include wireless Internet and a small fitness room. **Hotel Gander** (100 TransCanada Hwy., 709/256-3931 or 800/563-2988, www.hotelgander.com, $120-176 s or d) is older, but it has 152 rooms and suites, a **restaurant** (daily 7am-2pm and 5pm-9pm, $13-27), a lounge with entertainment, an indoor pool, and an exercise room.

Beside the Comfort Inn is **Jungle Jim's** (112 TransCanada Hwy., 709/651-3444, daily 11am-11pm, $13-22). If you can get the waitstaff's attention through the vines and bamboo decorations, order dishes such as fish-and-chips or ribs.

Getting There

It's almost 150 kilometers (1.5 hours) northwest to Gander from Clarenville via Route 1. From St. John's, it's a 340-kilometer (four-hour) drive on Route 1.

NORTH TO TWILLINGATE

From Gander, Route 330 heads north to Gander Bay, where Route 331 curves farther northwest and lopes onto the northern archipelago as Route 340, better known as the Road to the Shore.

Boyd's Cove

Boyd's Cove, 70 kilometers north of Gander, at the intersection of Routes 331 and 340, is a small village with a large attraction: **Beothuk Interpretation Site** (709/656-3114, mid-May-early Oct. daily 9:30am-5pm, adult $5). Designed to mimic the shapes of 300-year-old Beothuk dwellings, the center lies at the end of a two-kilometer gravel road. The detour is worth it, though, for the artifacts, dioramas, films, and exquisitely expressive paintings depicting the history of the Beothuk people. Take the 20-minute walk down to the site of the 17th-century Beothuk encampment, excavated in the early 1980s. Eleven house pits, clearly defined by earthen walls, were discovered here, along with countless artifacts, such as beads, stone tools, and iron.

GETTING THERE

From Gander, it's 70 kilometers (one hour) north to Boyd's Cove via Route 330 and Route 331. To get to Boyd's Cove from St. John's, it's a 410-kilometer (five-hour) drive on Route 1, 330, and 331.

TWILLINGATE

Beyond Boyd's Cove, causeways link an archipelago of islands lying close to the mainland. Along the way, narrow Route 430 passes farmland (where you might catch a glimpse of the rare Newfoundland pony); gentle, island-filled bays; and tiny outports to finish at South and North Twillingate islands. The archipelago's most northwesterly point, the islands are washed by the Atlantic and shouldered by Notre Dame Bay. The road crosses the southern island and eases into the tiny port at Twillingate Harbour.

Cross the causeway to Twillingate (pop. 3,500) on the northwestern island. Main Street runs alongside the scenic harbor before it zips north and climbs to Long Point.

Sights and Recreation

TWILLINGATE MUSEUM

If you're interested in local lore, stop at **Twillingate Museum** (1 St. Peter's Church Rd., 709/884-2825, mid-May-early Oct. daily 9am-9pm, adult $4, child $2). The white-washed wooden building sits back from the road and is bordered by a white picket fence—altogether as proper as a former Anglican manse should be. The museum's extensive exhibits include historic fishing gear and tools, antique dolls, and several rare Dorset Inuit artifacts. One room is devoted to the career of Dr. John Olds, Twillingate's famous expatriate surgeon who came from the United States to pioneer medicine in remote Newfoundland. The intriguing medical artifacts include a collection of early 20th-century pharmaceuticals and glass eyes.

★ ICEBERG-VIEWING

Icebergs, which wander offshore and sometimes ditch at land's end in Notre Dame Bay, are one of Twillingate's main claims to fame. If you're interested in getting up close, take one of the three daily cruises offered by **Twillingate Island Boat Tours** (50 Main St., 709/884-2242 or 800/611-2374, www.icebergtours.ca, adult $55, child $35), based at

icebergs off the coast of Twillingate

the Iceberg Shop, on the south side of the harbor (turn right as you enter town). Tours operate May-September, although the best iceberg viewing is late May-mid-June. Departures are daily at 9:30am, 1pm, and 4pm, and tours last two hours. They are operated by Cecil Stockley, who steers the MV *Iceberg Alley* to wherever icebergs have grounded in the vicinity of Twillingate.

You may also see an offshore iceberg from Back Harbour, a short walk starting from the museum and passing by a cemetery. Otherwise, head for Long Point, the high rocky promontory that juts into the Atlantic Ocean beside Notre Dame Bay. To get there, take Main Street around the harbor (past the museum and Harbour Lights Inn) and follow the road all the way to **Long Point** for the best land-based iceberg viewing in the area. In addition to a photogenic lighthouse, trails lead down through the boulder-strewn point and across to a couple of pebbly beaches.

Accommodations

Visitors to Twillingate often find themselves captivated by the town's charm, and because of this, numerous accommodations can be found. ★ **Harbour Lights Inn** (189 Main St., 709/884-2763, www.harbourlightsinn. ca, Apr.-late Oct., $120-155 s or d) is a restored early 19th-century home overlooking the harbor. The inn features nine guest rooms decorated in smart colors and appealing furnishings, each with an en suite bathroom and wireless Internet access; two rooms have whirlpool baths. Rates include a cooked breakfast.

If you prefer more privacy, consider **Cabins by the Sea** (11 Hugh Ln., 709/884-2158, www.cabinsbythesea.com, $89 s or d), comprising seven small self-contained cabins overlooking the ocean. If the timing is right, you may see icebergs from your cabin.

Getting There

To get to Twillingate from Boyd's Cove, take Route 340 north for 40 kilometers (40 minutes). From St. John's, it's a 445-kilometer

(six-hour) drive west on Route 1, then north on Route 330, 331, and 340.

GRAND FALLS-WINDSOR

For the sake of government, the two towns of Grand Falls-Windsor have been merged to form one municipality, but keep in mind that Windsor lies north of the TransCanada Highway and Grand Falls south. Grand Falls-Windsor lies almost exactly halfway along the Newfoundland leg of the TransCanada Highway: St. John's is 428 kilometers to the east, and Port-aux-Basques is 476 kilometers to the west.

Sights

Grand Falls offers the most sightseeing. Turn south off the highway at Cromer Avenue to the **Mary March Provincial Museum** (24 St. Catherine St., 709/292-4522, early May-Sept. Mon.-Sat. 9am-4:30pm, Sun. noon-4:30pm, adult $2.50), where exhibits about the area's Beothuk people, natural history, geology, and regional industry fill the modern center.

The town is aptly named for its **Grand Falls,** a white-water gush of rapids across the Exploits River as it speeds alongside the town. To see the falls, take Scott Avenue off the TransCanada Highway to the south and you'll find yourself in the heart of downtown Grand Falls. Cross the river at a narrow wooden bridge at the now-closed pulp and paper mill and look north for the best views. You can get a close look at the salmon that inhabit the river by continuing beyond the bridge to the **Salmonid Interpretation Centre** (709/489-7350, mid-June-mid-Sept. daily 8am to 8pm, adult $4, child $2.50). The main floor's exhibits explain the salmon's life cycle and habitat, while on the observation level you can watch the migratory salmon through the viewing windows.

Food

On the south side of the highway, the main street of Grand Falls offers a couple of reasonable dining options. Opposite the distinctively arched town hall entrance is **Daily Grind** (12 High St., 709/489-5252, Mon.-Wed. 7:30am-5pm, Thurs.-Fri. 7:30am-6pm,

Icebergs on Parade

The spectacular icebergs that float past Newfoundland and Labrador every summer originate from southwestern Greenland's ice cap, where great chunks of ice calve off the coast and cascade into the bone-chilling Davis Strait. The young bergs eventually drift out to the Labrador Sea, where powerful currents route them south along the watery route known as Iceberg Alley. The parade usually starts in March, peaks in June and July, and in rare cases continues into November.

Although no one actually counts icebergs, an educated guess has 10,000-30,000 of them migrating down from the north annually. Of those, about 1,400-2,000 make it all the way to the Gulf Stream's warm waters, where they finally melt away after a two- to four-year, 3,200-kilometer journey.

No two bergs are exactly the same. Some appear distinctly white. Others may be turquoise, green, or blue. Sizes vary too: A "growler" is the smallest, about the size of a dory, and weighs about 1,000 tons. A "bergy bit" weighs more, about 10,000 tons. A typical "small" iceberg looms 5-15 meters above water level and weighs about 100,000 tons. A "large" ice mass will be 51-75 meters high and weigh 100-300 million tons. Generally, you'll see the largest bergs—looking like magnificent castles embellished with towers and turrets—farther north; the ice mountains diminish in size as they float south and eventually melt. No matter what the size, what you see is just a fraction of the whole—some 90 percent of the iceberg's mass is hidden beneath the water.

Occasionally, a wandering berg may be trapped at land's edge or wedged within coves and slender bays. Should you be tempted to go in for a closer look, approach with caution. As it melts and its equilibrium readjusts, an iceberg may roll over. And melting bergs also often fracture, throwing ice chips and knife-sharp splinters in all directions.

The best website for information and tracking data is www.icebergfinder.com, which includes up-to-date satellite images of where icebergs are located.

Sat. 10am-5pm, lunches $6-9.50), with a great selection of coffees and teas, as well as light breakfasts and lunches. Down the hill slightly and across the road is **Tai Wan Restaurant** (48 High St., 709/489-4222, Tues.-Sat. 11am-2:30pm and 4:30pm-10pm, $9-14), filled with bright red and gold furnishings and walls decorated in local art. The lunch and dinner buffets are $10 and $13, respectively.

Accommodations

On the residential outskirts of Windsor, **Carriage House Inn** (181 Grenfell Heights, 709/489-7185 or 800/563-7133, www.carriagehouseinn.ca, $99-139 s or d) comprises 12 spick-and-span guest rooms, with full breakfast included in the rates. Outside you'll find a covered veranda, a pool, a sundeck, and gardens.

Mount Peyton Hotel (214 Lincoln Rd., 709/489-2251 or 800/563-4894, www.mountpeyton.com, $120-170 s or d) has an array of accommodations on both sides of the TransCanada Highway, including 102 hotel rooms, 32 motel rooms, and 16 housekeeping units. The motel's dining room is known locally for its seafood, locally grown vegetables, and dessert, made up of berries in all forms.

★ **Hotel Robin Hood** (78 Lincoln Rd., 709/489-5324, www.hotelrobinhood.com, $125-150 s or d) is Grand Falls-Windsor's most appealing motel. Small and charming, it's set off from the road and run by a couple from Nottingham, England. The 14 rooms, all air-conditioned and with private baths and larger flat-screen TVs, are comfortable and spacious. Rates include a continental breakfast.

Information

The best planning tool for visiting the area is the **Town of Grand Falls-Windsor** website (www.grandfallswindsor.com).

Getting There

Grand Falls and Windsor are just shy of 100 kilometers (one hour) west of Gander via Route 1. From St. John's, it's a 440-kilometer, five-hour drive northwest on Route 1.

Deer Lake to Port-aux-Basques

It's 270 kilometers from the western hub of Deer Lake south to the ferry terminal at Port-aux-Basques. Along the way is Newfoundland's second-largest city, Corner Brook; Atlantic Canada's premier ski resort; and many interesting provincial parks and scenic detours.

DEER LAKE

Deer Lake, 640 kilometers west of St. John's and 270 kilometers from Port-aux-Basques, is a busy transportation hub at the point where Route 430 spurs north along the Northern Peninsula. The town lies at the north end of its namesake lake, a long body of water that flows into the Humber River. Along the lakeshore is a sandy beach and shallow stretch of water that offers pleasant swimming in July and August. The only commercial attraction is the **Newfoundland Insectarium** (2 Bonne Bay Rd., 709/635-4545, mid-May-June and Sept.-mid-Oct. daily 9am-5pm, July-Aug. daily 9am-6pm, adult $12, senior $10, child $8). Inside this converted dairy, displays include active beehives and a collection of butterflies. To get there, take Exit 16 from the TransCanada Highway and follow Route 430 for a short distance to Bonne Bay Road.

Sir Richard Squires Provincial Park

Take Route 430 for eight kilometers to reach the turnoff to the remote **Sir Richard Squires Provincial Park,** which is then a further 47 kilometers from civilization. The park protects a short stretch of the upper reaches of the Humber River; salmon are the main draw. Even if you're not an angler, watching them leap up three-meter-high Big Falls in late summer makes the drive worthwhile. Camping is $18 per night.

Accommodations and Camping

Deer Lake Motel (15 TransCanada Hwy., 709/635-2108 or 800/563-2144, www.deerlakemotel.com, $120-160 s or d) is your typical low-slung roadside motel; the standard rooms are midsized, but comfortable and regularly revamped. This motel also has a restaurant with dinner mains in the $14-24 range, and a small lounge.

Take the Nicholsville Road exit to reach **Deer Lake RV Park** (197 Nicholsville Rd., 709/635-5885, www.dlrvparkandcampground.com, late June-early Sept., $24-29), close to the lake and with showers and a playground.

Information

Along the highway through town (beside the Irving gas station, with its big moose out front) is **Deer Lake Information Centre** (TransCanada Hwy., 709/635-2202, May-Oct. daily 8am-8pm), which has a number of displays on regional attractions and the Northern Peninsula.

Getting There

Deer Lake Airport (1 Airport Rd., 709/635-5270, www.deerlakeairport.com) is western Newfoundland's air hub. Located on the north side of town, just off the TransCanada Highway, it has Avis, Budget, Enterprise, Thrifty, and National car rental desks (make reservations well in advance). The airport is served by **Air Canada** (888/247-2262) from Halifax and Montréal, **WestJet** (888/937-8538) to Toronto and **PAL Airlines** (709/576-3943 or 800/563-2800, www.provincialairlines.ca) from throughout Newfoundland and Labrador.

Deer Lake is about 215 kilometers (2.5 hours) west of Grand Falls-Windsor on Route 1. From the ferry terminal in

The Beothuks

Across the island's central area, the arrival of Europeans foretold grave consequences for the Beothuks, who had migrated from Labrador in AD 200 and spread across the Baie Verte Peninsula to Burnside, Twillingate, and the shores of the Exploits River and Red Indian Lake.

In 1769, a law prohibiting murder of the indigenous people was enacted, but the edict came too late. The Beothuks were almost extinct, and in 1819 a small group was ambushed by settlers near Red Indian Lake. In the ensuing struggle, a 23-year-old woman named Demasduit was captured, and her husband and newborn infant were killed. The government attempted to return her to her people when she contracted tuberculosis, but she was too ill, and she died in Botwood. In 1823, her kinswoman, Shanawdithit, was also taken by force. Shanawdithit told a moving tale of the history and demise of her people, punctuating it with drawings, maps, and a sampling of Beothuk vocabulary before she died in 1829, the last of her race.

You'll hear mention of the Beothuks throughout central Newfoundland, but two attractions concentrate on these almost mythical people—the **Beothuk Interpretation Site** (709/656-3114, mid-May-early Oct. daily 9:30am-5pm, adult $5), 70 kilometers north of Gander on the road to Twillingate, and Grand Falls' **Mary March Provincial Museum** (24 St. Catherine St., 709/292-4522, early May-Sept. Mon.-Sat. 9am-4:30pm, Sun. noon-4:30pm, adult $2.50), which is named for Demasduit's European given name.

Port-aux-Basques, it's about 270 kilometers (three hours) north to Deer Lake on Route 1.

CORNER BROOK AND VICINITY

Corner Brook, 50 kilometers southwest of Deer Lake and 690 kilometers from the capital, lies at the head of the Humber Arm, 50 kilometers inland from the Gulf of St. Lawrence. The city is picturesquely cupped in a 20-square-kilometer bowl sloping down to the water, but most of the best natural attractions lie outside city limits, including the area around Marble Mountain and along Route 450 to Lark Harbour. The city ranks as Newfoundland's second largest, combining Corner Brook (pop. 20,000) with outlying settlements on the Humber Arm (another 20,000). It began as a company town, developing around a harbor-front pulp and paper mill that's still in operation, and has grown to become western Newfoundland's commercial, educational, service, and governmental center.

Town Sights

Making your way down to the harbor front from the TransCanada Highway is simple enough, but to visit the main downtown sights, orient yourself by stopping at the **information center** and deciding exactly what you want to see and do.

Captain Cook's Monument is a lofty lookout with views that provide a feeling for the layout of the city. On the road to the monument, you'll be rewarded with glorious views as far as the Bay of Islands. Follow O'Connell Drive across town, turn right (north) on Bliss Street, make another right on Country Road, turn left onto Atlantic Avenue with another left to Mayfair Street, and then right to Crow Hill Road. The monument itself commemorates Cook's Bay of Islands explorations with a plaque and sample chart.

In the wide bowl containing downtown, West Valley Road roughly divides the city in half. Near the bottom end of this thoroughfare and overlooking Remembrance Square is the staid **Corner Brook Museum** (2 West St., 709/634-2518, summer Mon.-Fri. 9am-5pm, the rest of the year Mon.-Fri. 10am-noon and 1pm-4:30pm, adult $5, child $3), housed in a historic building that has served as a post office, courthouse, and customs house through the years. Displays center around the various local industries and their impact on the city's growth.

Corner Brook

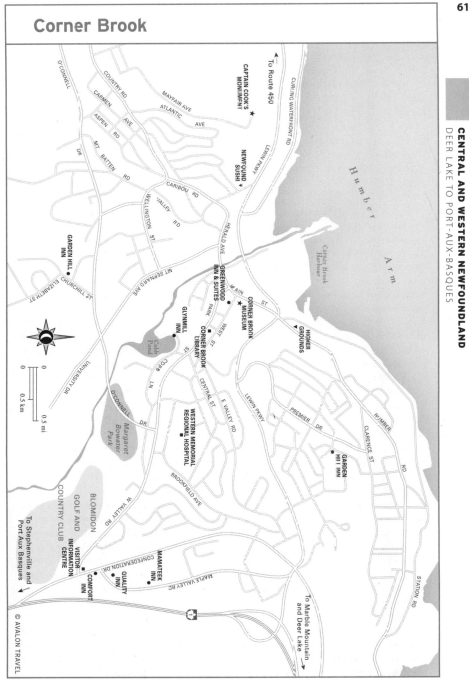

To Route 450

CAPTAIN COOK'S MONUMENT

NEWFOUND SUSHI

O'CONNELL

COUNTRY RD

MAYFAIR AVE

CARMEN AVE

ATLANTIC AVE

ASPEN RD

MT. BATTEN RD

CARIBOU RD

VALLEY RD

WELLINGTON ST

HERALD AVE

GARDEN HILL INN

MT. BERNARD AVE

CHURCHILL ST

ELIZABETH ST

CURLING WATERFRONT RD

LEWIN PKWY

Humber Arm

Corner Brook Harbour

GREENWOOD INN & SUITES

MAIN ST

CORNER BROOK MUSEUM

GLYNMILL INN

CORNER BROOK LIBRARY

PARK ST

WEST ST

Cobb Pond

COBB LN

UNIVERSITY DR

O'CONNELL DR

Margaret Bowater Park

CENTRAL ST

WESTERN MEMORIAL REGIONAL HOSPITAL

HIGHER GROUNDS

LEWIN PKWY

E VALLEY RD

PREMIER DR

HUMBER RD

CLARENCE ST

GARDEN HILL INN

0
0.5 km

0
0.5 mi

BROOKFIELD AVE

BLOMIDON GOLF AND COUNTRY CLUB

W VALLEY RD

VISITOR INFORMATION CENTRE

CONFEDERATION DR

COMFORT INN

QUALITY INN

MAMATEEK INN

MAPLE VALLEY RD

To Stephenville and Port Aux Basques

To Marble Mountain and Deer Lake

STATION RD

© AVALON TRAVEL

Marble Mountain

Driving south from Deer Lake, you pass **Marble Mountain** (709/637-7601, www.ski-marble.com), 12 kilometers before reaching Corner Brook. The mountain rises from the east side of the highway, while on the other side of the road is the small community of Steady Brook, which fronts the Humber River. The resort is Atlantic Canada's largest and best-known alpine resort, and although the lifts don't operate in summer, the area is worth a stop during the warmer months. The highlight is **Steady Brook Falls,** accessible via a steep-ish trail that begins from the far corner of the main parking lot. The falls are reached in about 15 minutes. From there, a 3.5-kilometer (one-way) unmarked trail continues and brings you nearer to the peak. The views of the Humber Valley and Bay of Islands are splendid.

Between December and April, four chairlifts, including a high-speed detachable quad, whisk skiers from throughout Atlantic Canada and as far away as Toronto up 520 vertical meters to access 27 runs, a terrain park, and a half-pipe. The base area is dominated by a magnificent four-story, 6,400-square-meter day lodge, home to a ski and snowboard school, rental shop, café, restaurant, and bar. Lift tickets are adult $60, senior $45, child $30. Check the website for packages that include accommodations.

Route 450

This winding highway follows the south shore of Humber Arm for 50 kilometers, ending at the fishing village of **Lark Harbour.** From the TransCanada Highway, Route 450 begins at Exit 4 and bypasses the city; from downtown, take the Lewin Parkway west to reach Route 450. Rather than official attractions, this drive is worthwhile for its water-and-mountains scenery and picturesque fishing villages.

Almost at the end of the road is **Blow Me Down Provincial Park.** The park isn't extraordinarily windy, as the name might imply. Legend holds that a sea captain saw the mountain centuries ago and exclaimed, "Well, blow me down." The name stuck. From the park, sweeping views across the Bay of Islands make the drive worthwhile. You'll see the bay's fjord arms and the barren orange-brown Blow Me Down Mountains, as well as bald eagles and ospreys gliding on the updrafts, and perhaps caribou and moose roaming the preserve's terrain. The remote park has 28 campsites ($18), pit toilets, a lookout tower, and hiking trails.

Food

Beyond the fast-food places along all the main arteries are some surprising dining options that require some searching out. **Higher Grounds** (9 Humber Rd., 709/639-1677, Mon.-Fri. 7:30am-6pm, Sat.-Sun. 9am-6pm, everything under $10) is an invitingly modern café with water views and free wireless Internet. Food is limited to soup and sandwiches, but the coffee and tea drinks are the best in town.

A real surprise in an otherwise unexceptional dining scene is ★ **Newfound Sushi** (117 Broadway, 709/634-6666, Tues.-Sat. 11am-2:30pm and 4pm-9pm, $12-24), away from the main street on the west side of downtown. The restaurant has just seven tables and a few seats along the sushi bar (or order takeout), but the modern decor and local art is appealing. The food itself is the main draw—a wonderful array of sushi and sashimi that takes full advantage of local seafood such as salmon, crab, and shrimp. Order individually or try the Dory Load of Sushi for two. For non-sushi eaters, there are stir-fries.

The Glynmill Inn (Cobb Ln., 709/634-5181) has two restaurants. The more formal and intimate of the two is the downstairs **Wine Cellar Steak House** (Mon.-Sat. from 6pm, $24-37), a cozy setting with a fine wine list. This dining room serves up some of the city's best unadorned beef, including grilled filet mignon served in 12-ounce cuts. Upstairs beside the lobby, the more casual **Carriage Room** (daily 7am-2pm and 5pm-9pm, $18-31) specializes in Newfoundland fare with standard cooked breakfasts and then fried, poached, or broiled salmon, cod, halibut, and lobster the rest of the day.

Accommodations and Camping

CORNER BROOK

With the exception of the historic Glynmill Inn, Corner Brook motels serve highway travelers and those in town on business. A scenic alternative is to stay out at Marble Mountain.

Garden Hill Inn (2 Fords Rd., 709/634-1150 or 888/534-1150, www.gardenhillinn.ca, $95-120 s or d) offers nine nonsmoking rooms, each with private bath and TV, in an attractive clapboard house with a large garden. Breakfast is included, and guests also have the use of a kitchen.

The gracious **Glynmill Inn** (Cobb Ln., 709/634-5181 or 800/563-4400, www.steelehotels.com, from $145 s or d) hosts two restaurants and lies near the historic Townsite residential area. It's a charming inn banked with gardens of red geraniums. Rambling ivy, with leaves as large as maple leaves, covers the half-timber Tudor-style exterior. The wide front steps lead to an open porch, and the English-style foyer is furnished with wing chairs and sofas. All the rooms are comfortably furnished, but the older ones feature old-time spaciousness and antique marble in the bathroom.

Quality Inn (64 Maple Valley Rd., 709/639-8901 or 800/563-8600, www.qualityinncornerbrook.com, from $135 s or d) has stunning views down to Humber Arm from many of the 55 guest rooms, which have undergone major renovations over the last few years. Rooms at the adjacent **Comfort Inn** (41 Maple Valley Rd., 709/639-1980 or 800/228-5150, www.choicehotels.ca, $120 s or d) are not as nice, but are a few dollars cheaper.

Greenwood Inn & Suites (48 West St., 709/634-5381 or 800/399-5381, www.greenwoodcornerbrook.com, from $150 s or d) is right downtown and across the road from Shez West, the best place in the city to sample Newfoundland cuisine. This full-service hostelry with regularly renovated guest rooms has its own English-style pub with sidewalk tables, an indoor heated pool, wireless Internet access, and underground parking.

MARBLE MOUNTAIN

Across the highway from Marble Mountain, 12 kilometers northeast of Corner Brook, is ★ **Marble Inn** (21 Dogwood Dr., Steady Brook, 709/634-2237 or 877/497-5673, www.marbleinn.com), a modern riverside complex that combines regular motel rooms (from $145 s or d) with luxurious two-bedroom suites overlooking the river ($295 s or d). Amenities include an indoor pool, a fitness room, spa services, a café, and a small restaurant open Tuesday-Saturday at 5pm for dinner (mains $18-48).

Also at Steady Brook is **Marble Villa** (709/637-7601 or 800/636-2725, www.ski-marble.com, $139-249 s or d), which is right at the base of the alpine resort. Some units have separate bedrooms; all have cooking facilities and wireless Internet. Naturally, winter is high season, when most guests stay as part of a package. In summer, the self-contained units rent from $139 s or d.

George's Mountain Village (709/639-8168, www.georgesskiworld.com) has a limited number of campsites under the shadow of Marble Mountain. It's part of a complex that includes a restaurant, gas station, and sports shop. Powered sites are $35 (although are not really suitable for larger RVs), and cabins with kitchens and separate bedrooms are $139 s or d.

Information and Services

Take Exit 5 or 6 from the TransCanada Highway and follow the signs to the **Visitor Information Centre** (11 Confederation Dr., 709/639-9792, daily Mon.-Fri. 8:30am-4:30pm, longer hours in summer), which is easily recognizable by its lighthouse-shaped design.

Western Memorial Regional Hospital (709/637-5000) is at 1 Brookfield Avenue. For the **RCMP**, call 709/637-4433.

Getting There and Around

Deer Lake, an hour's drive north of Corner Brook, has the region's main airport. **DRL-LR** (709/634-7422, www.drl-lr.com) operates bus service along the TransCanada

Highway, with daily stops in Corner Brook (at the Confederation Dr. Irving gas station). Departures from St. John's at 8am arrive in Deer Lake at 5:15pm.

If you're coming up from the ferry at Port-aux-Basques, allow around two hours for the 220-kilometer trip north on Route 1. Corner Brock is 50 kilometers (one hour) southwest of Deer Lake on Route 1.

The city has half a dozen cab companies whose cabs wait at lodgings, cruise business streets, and take calls. **City Cabs** (709/634-6565) is among the largest outfits.

STEPHENVILLE AND VICINITY

With a population of more than 8,000, Stephenville, 50 kilometers south of Corner Brook and then 40 kilometers west along Route 460, is the business hub for the Bay St. George-Port au Port region. In the center of town is **Winterhouse** (108 Main St., 709/643-4844), renowned for Winterhouse sweaters ($120-175), designed locally and produced by cottage-industry knitters. The shop is also a source for thrummed mittens ($20-35) and caps. This revived traditional craft combines a knitted woolen facing backed with raw fleece. The shop shelves are stuffed with top-quality wares, including Woof Design sweaters, Random Island Weaving cotton placemats, King's Point Pottery platters and bowls, and handmade birch brooms.

Barachois Pond Provincial Park

One of western Newfoundland's most popular parks, 3,500-hectare **Barachois Pond Provincial Park** is beside Route 1 west of Stephenville. It is home to a 3.2-kilometer hiking trail through birch, spruce, and fir trees to Erin Mountain's barren summit (the trailhead is within the campground). Be on the lookout for the rare Newfoundland pine marten along the way. The view at the 340-meter summit extends over the Port au Port Peninsula. There's also a summertime interpretive program

with guided walks and evening campfires, a lake for swimming and fishing, and 150 unserviced campsites ($18).

Accommodations

Stephenville offers a selection of downtown hotels and restaurants to travelers heading out onto the Port au Port Peninsula. The best of these is **Dreamcatcher Lodge** (14 Main St., 709/643-6655 or 888/373-2668, www.dreamcatcherlodge.ca, $110-130 s or d), at the far end of the main street through downtown. It comprises three buildings filled with a mix of motel rooms and kitchen-equipped units.

Getting There

Stephenville is 170 kilometers (two hours) north of Port-aux-Basques on Route 1.

STEPHENVILLE TO PORT-AUX-BASQUES

Most northbound travelers, having just arrived in Newfoundland (and southbound travelers heading to the ferry) don't plan on lingering along the stretch of highway between Stephenville and Port-aux-Basques, but the detour into the Codroy Valley, 39 kilometers north of Port-aux-Basques, is worthwhile. Near the main highway is the **Wetland Interpretation Centre** (Rte. 406, Upper Ferry, 709/955-2109, June-early Sept. daily 9am-5pm, free), where you can learn about the 300 bird species recorded in the valley, including great blue herons who are at the northern extent of their range. You can also ask for free bird checklists and a map showing the best viewing spots. Continue west to reach **Codroy Valley Provincial Park,** protecting a stretch of coastline including grass-covered sand dunes and a long sandy beach facing Cabot Strait. The highlight for birders is the chance to spot shorebirds such as piping plovers (late spring-midsummer).

Cape Anguille

Continue west beyond the provincial park along Route 406 to reach Cape Anguille, where ★ **Cape Anguille Lighthouse**

Inn (Rte. 406, 709/634-2285 or 877/254-6586, www.linkumtours.com, May-Oct., $120-130 s or d) sits high above a rugged shoreline. The lighthouse itself is still in use, but the lighthouse keeper (who was born out here) has opened up a few simple rooms for guests in a trim red-and-white cottage adjacent to the main lighthouse. Breakfast is included, and a highly recommended dinner of local specialties ($30 pp) is available with advance notice.

Port-aux-Basques

Just over 900 kilometers from its starting point in St. John's, the TransCanada Highway reaches its western terminus at Port-aux-Basques, a town of about 5,000 with a deep-water port used by French, Basque, and Portuguese fishing fleets as early as the 1500s. Arriving in town from the north, the main highway continues two kilometers to the ferry terminal, and a side road branches west, past hotels and fast-food restaurants to the township proper.

ACCOMMODATIONS AND CAMPING

Just over two kilometers from the ferry terminal is **Shark Cove Suites** (16 Currie Ave., 709/695-3831, $95 s or d), a small complex of simple units. Each has a kitchen and a lounge with a TV/DVD combo. Originally a Holiday Inn, **Hotel Port aux Basques** (2 Grand Bay Rd., 709/695-2171 or 877/695-2171, www.hotel-port-aux-basques.com, $119-169 s or d) sits on the corner where the highway branches to the ferry terminal. The restaurant has a fair selection of local delicacies at reasonable prices (seafood dishes $14-23), and the hotel also has a lounge.

If you're camping, your best choice is six kilometers north of town, at **J. T. Cheeseman Provincial Park,** where more than 100 sites ($18-27) are spread along a picturesque stream. Facilities are limited, but the park is fronted by a long beach and is a nesting ground for the endangered piping plover.

INFORMATION

Housed in a distinctive pyramid-shaped building just north of the turnoff to town is a provincial **Visitor Information Centre** (709/695-2262, May-Oct. daily 9am-8pm and for all ferry arrivals).

GETTING THERE

Port-aux-Basques is 170 kilometers (two hours) south of Stephenville via Route 1.

sunset along the coast south of the Codroy Valley

Port-aux-Basques is the northern terminus of year-round **Marine Atlantic** (902/794-5254 or 800/341-7981, www.marineatlantic.ca) ferry service from North Sydney (Nova Scotia). It's the shorter and less expensive of the two crossings to Newfoundland from North Sydney. One-way fares and rates for the five- to seven-hour sailing are adult $44, senior $40, child $20, vehicle under 20 feet $115. Extras include reserved chairs in a private lounge ($12-20) and cabins ($130-170).

Gros Morne National Park

UNESCO World Heritage Sites are scattered across the world. Egypt boasts the pyramids. France is known for Chartres Cathedral. Australia has the Great Barrier Reef. And Newfoundland boasts 1,085-square-kilometer Gros Morne National Park, a spectacular geological slice of the ancient world.

Gros Morne is on Newfoundland's west coast, 72 kilometers northwest from the town of Deer Lake. While the geological history will amaze you, there's also a wealth of hiking and boating tours and cross-country skiing in winter. Even though the park is remote, it is surrounded by small towns that cater to visitors, with lodging and restaurants to suit all budgets. There's even a dinner theater.

The Land

The park fronts the Gulf of St. Lawrence on a coastal plain rimmed with 70 kilometers of coast, edging sandy and cobblestone beaches, sea stacks, caves, forests, peat bogs, and breathtaking saltwater and freshwater fjords. The flattened Long Range Mountains, part of the ancient Appalachian Mountains, rise as an alpine plateau cloaked with black and white spruce, balsam fir, white birch, and stunted tuckamore thickets. Bare patches of peridotite, toxic to most plants, speckle the peaks, and at the highest elevations, the vegetation gives way to lichen, moss, and dwarf willow and birch on the arctic tundra.

Innumerable moose, arctic hares, foxes, weasels, lynx, and a few bears roam the park. Two large herds of woodland caribou inhabit the mountains and migrate to the coastal plain during winter. Bald eagles, ospreys, common and arctic terns, great black-backed gulls, and songbirds nest along the coast, while rock ptarmigans inhabit the mountain peaks. You might see willow ptarmigans on the lower slopes or, especially during the June-early July capelin run, a few pilot, minke, or humpback whales offshore.

Park Entry

Gros Morne National Park is open year-round, although all but one campground and the two information centers operate only in the warmer months. A **National Parks Day Pass** is adult $10, senior $8.50, child $5, to a maximum of $20 per vehicle. It is valid until 4pm the day following its purchase. A **Viking Trail Pass** (adult $45, senior $36, child $24) is valid for park entry and admission to Northern Peninsula national historic sites for seven days from the date of purchase. Passes can be purchased at the information center at Rocky Harbour or the Discovery Centre at Woody Point.

ROUTE 430

This is the main route up the Northern Peninsula. From Wiltondale, it's 86 kilometers to the park's northern extremity; from Rocky Harbour, it's 51 kilometers. The highway traverses terrain typical of the island's rocky seacoast and verdant hills and mountains, a distinct contrast to the southern area. Unusual groups of faulted and folded rock layers lie along this coastline.

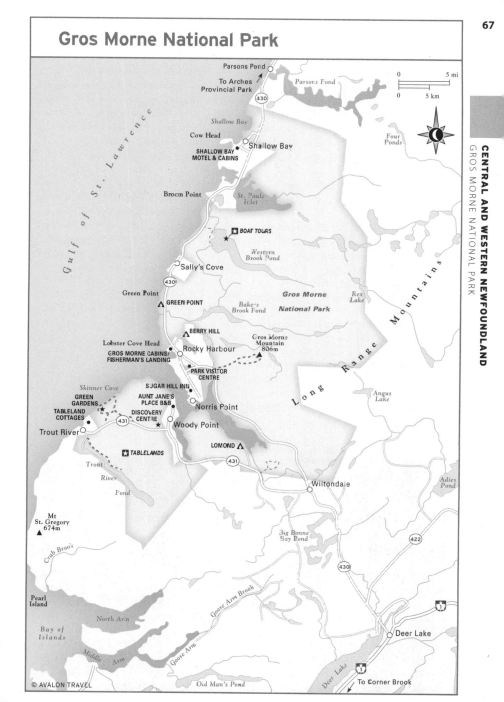

Gros Morne National Park

© AVALON TRAVEL

Lobster Cove Head

The point of land north of Rocky Harbour is Lobster Cove Head. Its layers formed as the North American plate slid beneath the eastern Eurasian/African plate 450-500 million years ago. Exhibits inside **Lobster Cove Head Lighthouse** (late May-mid-Oct. daily 10am-5:30pm, free) depict local lore, geological facts, and ancient natural history, but the views from outside are what make a visit worthwhile, especially as the sun sets over Bonne Bay and the Gulf of St. Lawrence beyond.

Rocky Harbour to Cow Head

More dramatically formed coastal rock lies farther north. **Green Point,** 17 kilometers beyond Lobster Cove, presents a tilted, textured surface of ribbon limestone and shale embedded with fossils from the Cambrian and Ordovician periods.

Continuing north, you'll come to the parking lot for the short trail to Western Brook Pond. One kilometer farther is where Western Brook drains into the Gulf of St. Lawrence. You'll find a sandy beach and an oceanfront picnic area. The headland immediately to the north is **Broom Point.** Along the access road is a platform and telescope, which you can train on the mountains that rise from Western Brook Pond.

Cow Head

Cow Head, 10 kilometers north of Broom Point, features an angled formation similar to that of Green Point, with limestone breccia (jumbled limestone chunks and fossils) spread across a small peninsula. The areas are richly textured. At Cow Head, the breccia looks like light-colored rock pillows scattered across a dark rock surface, while Green Point's surface is a rich green and textured like crushed velvet. The rock layers at both places originated during deepwater avalanches as the Iapetus Ocean formed 460-550 million years ago. In the village itself, beside **St. Mary's Church,** is a small botanical garden.

ROUTE 431

From Wiltondale, 31 kilometers north of Deer Lake, Route 431 leads west, entering the park after 13 kilometers.

Discovery Centre

If you've entered Gros Morne on Route 431, make your first stop the **Discovery Centre** (709/458-2417, mid-May-June and Sept.-early Oct. daily 9am-5pm, July-Aug. daily

Moose are common throughout Gros Morne National Park.

Lobster Cove Head Lighthouse

9am-6pm, included in park entry fee), on the hill above Woody Point. This modern facility showcases everything the national park is renowned for. The main display area holds an impressive 3-D map of the park, geological samples and descriptions, a human history display, and a theater. A gift shop sells park literature, and a café specializes in regional cuisine. Outside, a short trail leads through a garden planted with species native to the park.

★ Tablelands

The **Tablelands,** the park's most prized geological tract, lies along Route 431, halfway between Woody Point and Trout River. It's an odd sight, more resembling Hudson Bay's bleached brown barrens than verdant Newfoundland. The 12-by-7-kilometer chunk once lay beneath the ancient Iapetus Ocean. Violent internal upheavals eventually thrust the unearthly landscape to the surface. The parched yellow and tan cliffs and boulders that resulted are formed of peridotite, an

igneous rock found in the earth's mantle. You can get a good idea of the landscape from the parking lot, but I encourage you to take a stroll along the easy Tablelands Trail. It's four kilometers each way, but you only need walk a short way to get a feeling for the starkness of the moonlike terrain.

Trout River

After leaving the Tablelands behind, Route 431 descends to the small fishing village of **Trout River,** on a protected bay 18 kilometers from Woody Point. A boardwalk rims the stony beach, leading past weather-worn wooden buildings to the mouth of the Trout River, where wharves are filled with lobster pots and fishing gear. Fronting the boardwalk are historic buildings open to the public, including the bright yellow 1898 Jacob A. Crocker House. Across the river, turn right over the bridge and look for a small sign on the left. This marks the start of a short trail (10 minutes round-trip) leading to the Old Man, a rock stack that is visible from town.

RECREATION

More than 100 kilometers of marked and unmarked hiking trails lead novice to expert trekkers into the park's nooks and crannies. Several privately operated boat tours probe the fjords. A provincial fishing license (available at any sports store) opens up angling for brook trout and arctic char on the fast-flowing streams and rivers.

If you'd like to know more about Gros Morne's natural history and geology, plan on attending a scheduled interpretive program and evening campfire talk; see the information center for a schedule.

Hiking

Even if you're not a keen hiker, you can enjoy short interpretive walks at **Broom Point** (32 kilometers north of Rocky Harbour) and the **Tablelands,** as well as the two-kilometer circuit of **Lobster Cove Head.** If you're planning on taking a boat tour on Western Brook Pond, you'll need to lace up your hiking boots for the three-kilometer walk to the dock. But it's the following two longer hikes that get most of the attention.

Between the Tablelands and Trout River are two trailheads for the **Green Gardens.** This feature originated as lava from erupting volcanoes in the Iapetus Ocean. The longer option (16 kilometers round-trip; allow six hours) begins from Route 431 on the west side of the Tablelands. Four kilometers farther west is another trailhead for the Green Gardens. This is a nine-kilometer loop (four hours). Regardless of which trail you take, the trails emerge on a high headland cloaked in rich green grasses overlooking the gulf. Below the headland, sea stacks and sea caves (accessible only at low tide) rise from the beach floor beside cliffs pocked with pillow lava, the solidified remnants of molten rock from 100 kilometers beneath the ancient seafloor.

Feeling fit? If so, the hike to the 806-meter bald summit of **Gros Morne Mountain** (eight kilometers one-way; allow eight hours for the round-trip) may be what you're looking for. Beginning from Route 430, just east of the main information center, the first hour's walking is across flat terrain. Tightly packed boulders mark the beginning of the actual ascent, which takes 2-2.5 hours. Unexpectedly, the trail empties at a corner of the flattened peak. The air is clear and exhilarating, but surprisingly chilly. Far below, climbers scramble fitfully up the rocky ascent. To the west rise the Long Range Mountains. Looking south, you'll see a sapphire fjord, laid like an angled ribbon across the green woodlands. The summit is bare shale, limestone, and quartzite rock sprinkled with wild grass tufts. Check weather forecasts before heading out, and carry raingear, a first-aid kit, and extra food, clothing, and drinking water.

If you're not entirely comfortable undertaking longer hikes within the park, consider joining a group organized by **Gros Morne Adventures** (709/458-2722 or 800/685-4624, www.grosmorneadventures.com), which charges $125 per person for a day hike.

★ Boat Tours

Like Scandinavia, Gros Morne National Park is famous for fjords, fringed sea arms carved by the last ice sheet and shouldered by forests and cliffs. Unlike their Scandinavian counterparts, the most spectacular are actually landlocked fjord lakes and are known as "ponds." These ponds—**Trout River, Ten**

the moonlike Tablelands

The Galápagos of Geology

"What the Galápagos are to biology, Gros Morne is to geology," declared Britain's Prince Edward when he visited and dedicated Gros Morne National Park as a UNESCO World Heritage Site in 1987.

Long before Newfoundland was an island, it was a landlocked part of a great supercontinent formed during Precambrian times. When the supercontinent broke apart, the land plates drifted, and a rift formed that filled with water—the Iapetus Ocean. After another 50 million years, give or take, the land plates reversed direction and moved toward each other. As the landmasses were pushed together, Newfoundland, not yet an island, perched high and dry near the center of another supercontinent. At that point, Newfoundland's only distinctive characteristic was a mountain rib—the budding Appalachian Mountains that now rim North America's eastern edge.

Strewn among the mountains now protected by Gros Morne National Park was a colossal geological heritage: remnants from the world's first supercontinent and parts of the Iapetus Ocean's seafloor. East of the mountains, the island's central plateau portion was made up of a great rectangular swatch of the crumpled ancient seabed, 200-250 kilometers in width and length.

Between then and now, the eons added a few more topographical touches. The retreating ice sheet uncovered the Labrador Trough, scooped out the Strait of Belle Isle, cut fjords into the coastlines, and pocked the interiors to create myriad lakes, such as spectacular Western Brook Pond.

Mile, Bakers Brook, and Western Brook—were carved by the ice sheets. But in each case, when the enormous ice sheet melted out, the coastline—which had been compressed by the sheer weight of the glacier—rebounded like a sponge, rising above sea level and cutting the fjord off from the sea.

Bontours (709/458-2016 or 888/458-2016, adult $58-65, child $20-25.50) offers a cruise on spectacular Western Brook Pond. Tickets can be booked by phone or in person at the Ocean View Motel in Rocky Harbour. To get to Western Brook Pond, you must drive 30 kilometers north from Rocky Harbour to a marked parking lot. From this point, it's a three-kilometer hike to the boat dock. During July and August, three tours depart daily (10am, 1pm, and 4pm), while in June and September there's just one tour daily (12:30pm). Plan on leaving Rocky Harbour at least 90 minutes before the scheduled departure time. This tour lasts two hours.

Other Tours

Gros Morne Adventures (709/458-2722 or 800/685-4624, www.grosmorneadventures.com) leads geology and natural-history tours through the park June-September.

The four-day backpacking adventure on the Long Range Traverse costs $1,295, inclusive of meals, permits, and camping accommodations. Kayaking is another specialty; a half day with instruction costs $125 per person, and kayak rentals from the company's Norris Point base cost $55-65 per day.

ENTERTAINMENT AND EVENTS

To immerse yourself in the culture of Newfoundland, plan on spending an evening at the Gros Morne Theatre Festival (709/639-7238, www.theatrenewfoundland.com, adult $30-45, child $13-25), which runs June-mid-September at Cow Head, 48 kilometers north of Rocky Harbour. The festival comprises two plays enacted by more than 40 professional actors, with performances that tell the story of people and events that have helped shape the province.

In Rocky Harbour, the Anchor Pub (Ocean View Hotel, Main St., 709/458-2730, daily 11:30am-close) has traditional Newfoundland music Monday, Wednesday, and Friday nights through summer. The cover charge is minimal and the small space gets surprisingly crowded.

FOOD

Rocky Harbour

If you rise early, head to ★ **Fisherman's Landing** (44 Main St., 709/458-2060, daily 6am-11pm, $13-23), across from the wharf, for a cooked breakfast special that includes juice and coffee. The rest of the day, it's traditional Newfoundland cooking at reasonable prices—grilled pork chops with baked potatoes and boiled vegetables, poached halibut, pan-fried cod tongues, and more. House wine is sold by the glass, but some bottles are under $25. A few tables have water views.

Cow Bay

Part of the Shallow Bay Motel complex, the **Bay View Family Restaurant** (193 Main St., 709/243-2471, daily 7am-9pm, $13-26) does indeed have bay views, but only from a few of the tables. Dining choices are as simple as a Newfie Mug (tea and molasses bread), but you can also order more recognizable meals, such as blackened salmon with Cajun spices and T-bone steaks.

Woody Point

The best two dining options are along the Woody Point waterfront. **Granite Coffee House** (Water St., 709/451-3236, daily from 7:30am, breakfasts $7-10) has a wide range of coffee drinks, as well as full cooked breakfasts and soup and sandwich specials. Upstairs in a converted warehouse, and with outdoor tables facing the water, **The Old Loft** (Water St., 709/453-2294, May-June and Sept. daily 11:30am-7pm, July-Aug. daily 11:30am-9pm, $12-23) is the best choice in town for lunch or dinner. Unlike many other Newfoundland restaurants, The Old Loft dishes up seafood choices that don't require a deep fryer in their preparation. The chowder is an excellent way to start, and if cheesecake is on the dessert menu, go for it.

Trout River

Along the waterfront in this end-of-the-road fishing village, the **Seaside Restaurant** (709/451-3461, mid-May-mid-Oct. daily noon-9pm, $12-24) enjoys sweeping water views. The restaurant has a reputation for consistently good food. The seafood chowder is overflowing with goodies, and fish-and-chips are cooked to perfection.

ACCOMMODATIONS

Rocky Harbour, 72 kilometers from Deer Lake, has the best choice of accommodations and is centrally located for exploring the park.

Rocky Harbour

Those not camping will find a variety of accommodations in Rocky Harbour, the park's major service area. For B&B accommodations, **Evergreen B&B** (4 Evergreen Ln., 709/458-2692 or 800/905-3494, www.grosmorne.ca/evergreen, $85 s, $95 d) has three guest rooms and a large patio with barbecue facilities. It's open year-round, and rates include a full breakfast.

The **Ocean View Hotel** (38 Main St., 709/458-2730 or 800/563-9887, www.theoceanview.ca, mid-Mar.-mid-Dec., from $149-269 s or d) enjoys a prime location across from the water in the heart of Rocky Harbour. Rooms in the older wing are high-quality and spacious, while those in the newer wing offer ocean views (from $169). The motel also has a downstairs bar with nightly entertainment, an upstairs restaurant, a booking desk for Western Brook Pond boat tours, and a super-funky old-fashioned elevator.

A short walk from the harbor, the units at **Mountain Range Cottages** (32 Parsons Ln., 709/458-2199, www.mountainrangecottages.com, mid-May-mid-Oct., $125-155 s or d) are an excellent value. Each of 10 simple but modern cottages has a full kitchen, a dining table, two separate bedrooms, a bathroom, and a balcony equipped with outdoor furniture and a barbecue.

Continue around the southern side of Rocky Harbour to reach ★ **Gros Morne Cabins** (Main St., 709/458-2020 or 888/603-2020, www.grosmornecabins.ca, $149-209 s or d), a modern complex of 22 polished log cabins strung out along the bay. Unfortunately, they don't take full advantage of the wonderful location (small windows and no balconies), but each has a kitchen, separate bedrooms, a propane barbecue, and wireless Internet. Other amenities include a playground and laundry, while part of the complex is a large general store.

Cow Head

In Cow Head, 48 kilometers north of Rocky Harbour, **Shallow Bay Motel and Cabins** (193 Main St., 709/243-2471 or 800/563-1946, www.shallowbaymotel.com, $105-145 s or d) lies close to long stretches of sandy beach, hiking trails, and Arches Provincial Park. The 68 guest rooms are basic but comfortable, and the 20 cabins have full kitchens. Amenities include a large restaurant and one of the only outdoor pools in western Newfoundland (don't worry, it's heated!).

Along Route 431

A luxurious lodging that seems a little out of place within this remote national park, **Sugar Hill Inn** (115 Sexton Rd., Norris Point, 709/458-2147 or 888/299-2147, www.sugarhillinn.ca, $185-255 s or d) is nevertheless a treat. The 11 guest rooms are accentuated with polished hardwood floors and earthy yet contemporary color schemes. The King Suites each have a vaulted ceiling, jetted tub, and sitting area with a leather couch. Breakfast is included in the rates, while dinner (mains $28-38) is extra. The inn is on the left as you descend to Norris Point.

One block back from the water in the heart of the village of Woody Point is **Aunt Jane's B&B** (1 Water St., 709/453-2485, www.grosmorneescapes.com, mid-May-mid-Oct., $70 s, $80-90 d), a charming 1880s home that contains five guest rooms, four with shared bathrooms. Aunt Jane's is one of numerous other guesthouses in town collectively marketed as **Victorian Manor Heritage Properties** (same contact). One of these is **Uncle Steve's,** a trim three-bedroom home with a kitchen and a TV lounge. It costs $235 per night, with a three-night minimum.

Trout River

At the end of Route 431 and a 10-minute walk along the river from the ocean, **Tableland Cottages** (709/451-2101, www.tablelandcottages.com, May-Oct., $130-160 s or d) has seven two-bedroom cottages, each with a small but workable kitchen.

CAMPING

Almost 300 campsites at five campgrounds lie within Gros Morne National Park. No electrical hookups are available, but each campground has flush toilets, fire pits (firewood costs $8 per bundle), at least one kitchen shelter, and a playground. All campgrounds except Green Point have hot showers.

A percentage of sites at all but Green Point can be reserved through **Parks Canada** (877/737-3783, www.pccamping.ca) for $11 per reservation—reassuring if you're visiting the park in the height of summer. The remaining sites fill on a first-come, first-served basis.

Route 430

Across Route 430 from Rocky Harbour, **Berry Hill Campground** (mid-June-early Sept., $19-26) has 69 sites, showers, kitchen shelters, and a playground. It fills quickly each summer afternoon, mostly with campers that have made advance reservations through Parks Canada, but also because of its central location.

The 31-site ★**Green Point Campground** ($16), 12 kilometers north of Rocky Harbour, is the only park campground open year-round, and it is the only one without showers. The oceanfront setting more than makes up for a lack of facilities.

At the park's northern extremity, **Shallow Bay Campground** (early June-mid-Sept., $19-26) offers full facilities and 62 sites within walking distance of the services of a small town.

Route 431

Lomond Campground (mid-May-early Oct., $19-26) edges Bonne Bay's east arm. It is popular with anglers but also is the start of three short walking trails, including one along the Lomond River.

Turn left at the end of Route 431 to reach **Trout River Pond Campground** (early June–mid-Sept., $19-26), which is close to the Trout River boat tour dock. It's only a small facility (44 sites), but it has a beautiful setting, hot showers, a playground, and wireless Internet.

INFORMATION AND SERVICES

The **Park Visitor Centre** (Rte. 430, 709/458-2417, mid-May-June and early Sept.-mid-Oct. daily 9am-5pm, July-early Sept. daily 8am-8pm) stocks literature, sells field guides, presents slide shows, and has exhibits on the park's geology, landscapes, and history. Outside is a telescope for a close-up view of Gros Morne Mountain. The center is along Route 430, just before the turnoff to Rocky Harbour.

The **Discovery Centre** (Route 431, 709/458-2417, mid-May-June and Sept.-early Oct. daily 9am-5pm, July-Aug. daily 9am-6pm) is another source of park information. For pre-trip planning, go to the **Parks Canada** website (www.pc.gc.ca) or check out the business links at www.grosmorne.com.

GETTING THERE AND AROUND

The nearest airport is in Deer Lake, 72 kilometers from Rocky Harbour. It is served by **Air Canada** (888/247-2262) from Halifax and Montréal. Car rental companies with airport desks include Avis, Budget, Enterprise, National, and Thrifty. Each allows 200 free kilometers per day, meaning you'll be unlikely to rack up extra charges on a trip to the park.

To get to Rocky Harbour from Deer Lake, head northwest on Route 430 for 72 kilometers (50 minutes). From the ferry terminal in Port-aux-Basques, it's about 340 kilometers (four hours) north to Rocky Harbour via Route 1 and Route 430.

Gros Morne National Park backcountry camping

Northern Peninsula

North of Gros Morne National Park, the Northern Peninsula sweeps northeast across mountainous, flat-topped barrens and ends in tundra strewn with glacial boulders. Route 430 (also known as the **Viking Trail**) runs alongside the gulf on the coastal plain and extends the peninsula's full length, finishing at St. Anthony, 420 kilometers north of Deer Lake.

As you drive this stretch of highway, you'll notice, depending on the time of year, either small black patches of dirt or tiny flourishing vegetable gardens lining the road. These roadside gardens belong to the people of the nearby villages; because of the region's nutrient-poor soil, people plant their gardens wherever they find a patch of fertile ground.

NORTH FROM GROS MORNE

Arches Provincial Park

Right beside the highway, just north of Gros Morne National Park, the intriguing geological feature known as **Arches Provincial Park** is well worth the drive, even if you're not planning on traveling up the Northern Peninsula. Two arches have been eroded into a grassed rock stack that sits along the rocky beach. At low tide you can climb underneath, but most visitors are happy to just stand back and snap a picture.

Daniel's Harbour

About 15 kilometers north of Arches Provincial Park is the village of **Daniel's Harbour.** It has an interesting little harbor and historic buildings such as the Nurse Myra Bennett Heritage House, once home to a woman known throughout Newfoundland and Labrador as the "Florence Nightingale of the North" for her medical exploits.

On the south side of town is **Bennett Lodge** (Rte. 430, 709/898-2211, www.bennettlodge.com, May-Oct., $95-105 s or d),

nothing more than a modular motel with a restaurant and dimly lit lounge. But it's one of the least expensive motels on the Northern Peninsula and has ocean views through the small guest room windows.

PORT AU CHOIX

About 160 kilometers north of Rocky Harbour, a road spurs west off Route 430 for 10 kilometers to Port au Choix, a small fishing village with a human history that dates back more than 4,500 years. The historic site related to these early residents is the town's main attraction, but the local economy revolves around the ocean and cold-water shrimp (those tasty little shrimp you see in salads and the like).

Port au Choix National Historic Site

The Maritime Archaic people and the later Dorset and Groswater Inuit migrated from Labrador, roamed the Northern Peninsula, and then settled on the remote cape beyond the modern-day town of Port au Choix. Today the entire peninsula is protected, with trails leading to the various dig sites. Start your exploration of the **Port au Choix National Historic Site** at the **Visitor Reception Centre** (709/861-3522, mid-June-mid-Sept. daily 9am-5pm, adult $8, senior $6.60, child $4), which is signposted through town. Here, the three cultures are represented by artifacts, exhibits, and a reconstruction of a Dorset Inuit dwelling. Dig sites are scattered over the peninsula, with a 3.5-kilometer trail leading from the center to the most interesting site, Phillip's Garden. First discovered in the 1960s, archaeological digs here revealed Dorset dwellings and an incredible wealth of Maritime Archaic cultural artifacts buried with almost 100 bodies at three nearby burial grounds. The digs continue to this day, and through summer you can watch archaeologists doing their painstaking work (if you're lucky, you may even see them uncover an ancient artifact). Free guided hikes depart daily at 1pm. If you drive through town beyond the shrimp-processing plant, you pass an Archaic cemetery and a parking lot (from which Phillip's Garden is a little closer, 2.5 kilometers one-way).

Museum of Whales and Things

Along the main road into town, the small **Museum of Whales and Things** (709/861-3280, Mon.-Sat. 9am-5pm, donation) is the work of local Ben Ploughman, who has, as the name suggests, collected a 15-meter-long sperm whale skeleton, as well as other "things." In an adjacent studio, Ploughman makes and sells driftwood creations.

Food

As you cruise through town, it's difficult to miss the ★ **Anchor Café** (Fisher St., 709/861-3665, summer daily 9am-11pm, spring and fall daily 10am-10pm, $6.50-17), with its white ship's bow jutting out into the parking lot. With the cold-water shrimp plant across the road, this is the place to try the local delicacy ($6 for a shrimp burger). You can also eat like locals have done for generations (corned fish with sides of brewis, pork scrunchions, and a slice of molasses bread) or try a Moratorium Dinner (a reference to the cod-fishing ban), such as roast turkey. Also good is the cod and shrimp chowder.

Along the same road, the **Sea Echo Motel** (Fisher St., 709/861-3777, summer daily 7am-9pm, the rest of the year daily 7:30am-7:30pm, $12-23) has a nautically themed restaurant with similar fare, including fish cakes and cod tongues.

Accommodations

As the town of Port au Choix continues to unfold its rich archaeological heritage, it also continues to expand its visitor services. One of these is **Jeannie's Sunrise Bed and Breakfast** (84 Fisher St., 709/861-2254 or 877/639-2789, www.jeanniessunrisebb.com, $99-129 s or d), owned by lifelong Port au Choix resident Jeannie Billard. Each of the five rooms is bright and spacious and has its own TV. The less expensive rooms share a bathroom. Rates include a full breakfast, and dinner is available on request. Jeannie also offers a self-contained two-bedroom cottage for $129 per night.

Sea Echo Motel (Fisher St., 709/861-3777, www.seaechomotel.ca, $118-128 s or d, including breakfast) has 30 fairly standard motel rooms with wireless Internet, three cabins, a restaurant with lots of local seafood, and a lounge.

Getting There

Port au Choix is 160 kilometers (two hours) north of Rocky Harbour on Route 430. From the ferry terminal in Port-aux-Basques, it's 500 kilometers (six hours) driving north along Route 1 and Route 430 to Port au Choix.

PLUM POINT

Continuing up the Northern Peninsula, the first worthwhile stop north of Port au Choix is Plum Point, where archaeologists have found evidence of human habitation from 4,500 years ago. At Plum Point, 60 kilometers north of Port au Choix, Route 430 continues north and Route 432 spurs east toward Roddickton. The latter is the longer route to St. Anthony, but an abundance of moose makes it an interesting alternative.

Bird Cove

Although visited by Captain Cook in 1764 and settled permanently by Europeans in 1900, Plum Point's first residents made a home for themselves as early as 4,500 years ago. These Maritime Archaic people were prehistoric hunters and gatherers who spent summers on the edge of **Bird Cove.** The two adjacent village sites, discovered as recently as the 1990s, were rare because they presented archaeologists with an undisturbed look at life many thousands of years ago. Shell middens, spear points used to hunt sea mammals, and tools used for woodworking have all been excavated. A boardwalk with interpretive panels leads around the site. To get there, drive to the end of the road, loop left past the grocery store, and take the unpaved road on the right-hand side of the light brown house. The boardwalk is on the left, a little under one kilometer from the grocery store.

Dog Peninsula

Beyond the general store, stay right as the road loops around, and you soon find yourself at a bridge linking the **Dog Peninsula** to the mainland. The peninsula is laced with walking trails that follow the shoreline and pass through the remains of an 1880s settlement. You can complete the first loop (turn right at the far end of the bridge) in around 30 minutes, even with time spent skimming a few of the super-flat stones into Bird Cove.

Food and Accommodations

Between the highway and the ocean, **Plum Point Motel** (709/247-2533 or 888/663-2533, www.plumpointmotel.com, $110-120 s or d) has 40 motel rooms and 18 basic cabins with kitchenettes. With a few water-view tables, the in-house **restaurant** (daily 7am-9pm, $10-21) serves the usual array of island cooking, including salted cod for breakfast, soups and sandwiches for lunch, and deep fried seafood for dinner.

Getting There

Plum Point is about 60 kilometers (50 minutes) north of Port au Choix via Route 430. From the ferry terminal in Port-aux-Basques, it's about 550 kilometers (6.5-7 hours) north to Plum Point via Route 1 and Route 430.

The main highway up the Northern Peninsula, Route 430, continues north from Plum Point, but an abundance of moose makes Route 432, which spurs east toward Roddickton, an interesting albeit longer alternative.

ST. BARBE

St. Barbe, 20 kilometers north of Plum Point and 300 kilometers north of Deer Lake, is where ferries depart for Labrador. There's little to see or do in town, but accommodations are provided at the **Dockside Motel** (709/877-2444 or 877/677-2444, www.docksidemotel.nf.ca, $99-129 s or d), which isn't at the dock at all. Instead, it's on the road leading down to the waterfront. Rooms are basic but adequate, the 10 cabins have kitchens, and the simple in-house restaurant is open daily for breakfast, lunch, and dinner.

Getting There

St. Barbe is 20 kilometers (20 minutes) north of Plum Point via Route 430. From the ferry terminal in Port-aux-Basques, it's 580 kilometers (seven hours) north to St. Barbe via Route 1 and Route 430.

Catching the Ferry to Labrador

If you are planning on exploring the Labrador Straits region, make ferry reservations long before arriving in St. Barbe. The ticket office is at the Dockside Motel, and even with reservations, you'll need to check in before heading down to the dock. The ferry **MV Apollo** (866/535-2567, www.labradormarine.com) sails from St. Barbe once or twice daily between early May and early January. The crossing takes around two hours. The one-way fare is a reasonable vehicle and driver $36, extra adult $12, senior and child $10. Across the road from the Dockside Motel is a fenced compound with hookups for RVs and a drop-off area for those catching the ferry and not wanting to travel with full rigs.

ST. BARBE TO ST. ANTHONY

It's 110 kilometers between St. Barbe and St. Anthony. For the first 50 kilometers, Route 430 hugs the Strait of Belle Isle, passing a string of fishing villages clinging tenuously to the rocky coastline. Tourist services are minimal, but there are a couple of worthwhile stops, and you should take the time to wander through one or more of these outports to get a feeling for the sights, sounds, and smells that go with living along this remote stretch of coastline.

Deep Cove Wintering Interpretation Site

Just beyond the turnoff to the modern-day village of Anchor Cove is **Deep Cove Wintering Interpretation Site,** an observation platform and trail that leads to the site of an 1860s village where residents of Anchor Cove would spend the winter. Only the weathered remains of a few wooden homes are left, but the site is interesting as one of the rare cases of European seasonal migration. It takes about 10 minutes to reach the site from Route 430.

★ Thrombolites of Flowers Cove

The picturesque village of **Flowers Cove,** its low profile of trim homes broken only by the occasional church spire, lies 13 kilometers north of St. Barbe. Turn onto Burns Road from Route 430 to reach the red-roofed Marjorie Bridge. Beyond the bridge, a boardwalk leads along the cove to an outcrop of **thrombolites.** Resembling flower-shaped boulders, they are actually the remnants of algae and bacteria that have been dated at 650 million years old, making them among the earliest forms of life on earth. While the actual thrombolites are, of course, interesting, it is the complete lack of surrounding hype for what is one of the world's rarest fossils (the only other place they occur is on the remote west coast of Australia) that makes visiting the site even more unforgettable.

ST. ANTHONY

Although you will want to continue north to L'Anse aux Meadows, St. Anthony (pop. 2,300), 450 kilometers north of Deer Lake, is the last real town and a service center for the entire Northern Peninsula. Most attractions revolve around Dr. Wilfred Grenfell, a

The thrombolites of Flowers Cove are the world's oldest living organisms.

medical missionary from England who established hospitals along both sides of Labrador Straits in the late 1800s. His impact on St. Anthony was especially powerful. It was here, in 1900, that Grenfell built his first year-round hospital and established a medical mission headquarters. St. Anthony still serves as the center of operations for the International Grenfell Association, which continues to build hospitals and orphanages and funds other community endeavors across the country.

The main natural attraction is **Fishing Point Park,** through town. From this lofty point, you have the chance to spy whales or icebergs.

Grenfell Historic Properties

Start your discovery of everything Grenfell at the **Grenfell Interpretation Centre** (West St., 709/454-4010, July-Aug. daily 8am-5pm, Sept.-June Mon.-Fri. 8am-5pm, adult $10, senior $8, child $3). This large facility details Grenfell's many and varied accomplishments, from the establishment of his first hospital at Battle Harbour to the work of the association that carries his name today. Grenfell also helped foster financial independence for remote outports through profitable organizations such as **Grenfell Handicrafts,** which still produces hand-embroidered cassocks, fox-trimmed parkas, hooked rugs, and jackets that are sold at a gift shop across from the admissions desk of the Grenfell Interpretation Centre.

Exit the museum through the tearoom and you come across the tiny **Dock House Museum** (July-Aug. daily 10am-4pm, free). Displays here describe how Grenfell's ships were pulled from the water for repairs after long voyages to remote communities.

A tribute to the life and works of Dr. Grenfell lives in the **Jordi Bonet Murals,** impressive ceramic panels adorning the walls of the rotunda at the entrance to Curtis Memorial Hospital, which is across the road from the Grenfell Interpretation Centre.

Exhibits at the stately green-and-white **Grenfell House Museum** (July-Aug. daily 8am-5pm, Sept.-June Mon.-Fri. 8am-5pm, free with proof of paid admission to Interpretation Centre), his home for many years, describe Grenfell's home and family life. The home is on the far side of the hospital, a five-minute walk from the Interpretation Centre. A trail starting from behind the home leads to Tea House Hill, where viewing platforms provide sweeping harbor views.

Tours

As the gateway to Iceberg Alley, St. Anthony is the place to take to the water in a tour boat. **Northland Discovery** (709/454-3092 or 877/632-3747, late May-mid-Sept., adult $60, child $25) departs three times daily from behind the Grenfell Interpretation Centre. When there's a lack of icebergs (mid-June-Aug. is the best viewing period), the captain concentrates on searching out humpback, minke, and fin whales, as well as seabirds. The covered vessel is stable and has washrooms. The 2.5-hour tours include hot drinks.

Food

Drive through town to reach ★ **Lightkeeper's** (Fishing Point Rd., 709/454-4900, summer daily 11:30am-9pm, $16-32), which, true to its name, follows a red-and-white color scheme that extends all the way down to the salt and pepper shakers. Housed in a converted light-keeper's residence overlooking the ocean (you may spot icebergs June-Aug.). This tiered dining room is casual, although a little on the expensive side. Starters include crab claws with garlic butter, while mains are mostly from the ocean, including seafood.

Haven Inn (14 Goose Cove Rd., 709/454-9100, daily 7am-9pm, $13-19) has a small, bright dining room that catches the morning sun. Cooked breakfasts are $8 and predictable dinners, such as roast beef and mashed potatoes, are all under $20.

Accommodations

Fishing Point B&B (Fishing Point Rd., 709/454-3117 or 866/454-2009, from $110 s or d) is through town and within walking distance of Lightkeeper's, the best place to eat in town. Built in the 1940s, the converted fisherman's home is set right on the harbor and has three guest rooms with either private or en suite bathrooms. Rates include a full breakfast.

Haven Inn (14 Goose Cove Rd., 709/454-9100 or 877/428-3646, www.haveninn.ca, $105-147 s or d) has 30 rooms in various configurations on a slight rise off Route 430. Rooms are fairly standard, but each has a coffeemaker and hair dryer; the more expensive ones have water views and gas fireplaces. The in-house restaurant (daily from 7am) dishes up inexpensive breakfasts.

A converted 1915 nursing residence that has been extensively renovated, **Grenfell Heritage Hotel** (1 McChada Dr., 709/454-8395 or 888/450-8398, www.grenfellheritagehotel.ca, $130-170 s or d) is the town's newest lodging, but it's also the most expensive. Rooms are simple but clean and comfortable. Kitchenettes, a free continental breakfast, and a handy waterfront location are all pluses.

Getting There

It's 110 kilometers (1.5 hours) from St. Barbe to St. Anthony going north and then east on Route 430. From the ferry terminal in Port-aux-Basques, it's about 690 kilometers (9.5 hours) north to St. Anthony via Route 1 and Route 430.

★ L'ANSE AUX MEADOWS

At the very end of Route 436 lies L'Anse aux Meadows, 48 kilometers from St. Anthony and as far as you can drive up the Northern Peninsula. It was here that the Vikings came ashore more than 1,000 years ago—the first Europeans to step foot in North America. Two Viking attractions make the drive worthwhile, but there's also a fine restaurant and lots of wild and rugged scenery.

L'Anse aux Meadows National Historic Site

Long before archaeologists arrived, Newfoundlanders were aware of the odd-shaped sod-covered ridges across the coastal plain at L'Anse aux Meadows. George Decker, a local fisherman, led Norwegian scholar-explorer Helge Ingstad and his wife, archaeologist Anne Stine Ingstad, to the area in the 1960s. The subsequent digs uncovered eight complexes of rudimentary houses, workshops with fireplaces, and a trove of artifacts, which verified the Norse presence. National recognition and site protection followed, leading to the creation of the **L'Anse aux Meadows National Historic Site** in 1977 and to UNESCO designating it a World Heritage Site the following year.

A **Visitor Reception Centre** (Rte. 436, 709/623-2608, June and Sept.-early Oct. daily 9am-5pm, July-Aug. daily 9am-6pm, adult $12, senior $10, child $6) has been developed above the site. Here you can admire excavated artifacts, view site models, and take in an audiovisual presentation. A gravel path and boardwalk lead across the grassy plain to the site of the settlement, where panels describe the original uses of buildings now marked by depressions in the grass-covered field. Just beyond is a settlement of re-created buildings overlooking Epaves Bay. Costumed interpreters reenact the roles and work of the Norse captain, his wife, and four crew members.

L'Anse aux Meadows National Historic Site

Norstead

Just beyond the turnoff to L'Anse aux Meadows National Historic Site is **Norstead** (Rte. 436, 709/623-2828, mid-June-mid-Sept. daily 9am-5pm, adult $10, senior $8, child $6.50), the re-creation of a Viking port of trade. Aside from the Viking theme, it has little resemblance to how the Vikings of L'Anse aux Meadows lived, but it is still well worth visiting. Right on the water, you can see a full-size replica of a Viking ship, listen to stories in the dimly lit Chieftains Hall, watch a blacksmith at work, and sample bread as it comes from the oven in the dining hall. The costumed interpreters bring this place to life, and you can easily spend an hour or more listening and watching them at work and play.

Food

Amazingly, at the end of the road is one of the finest dining rooms in all of Newfoundland, the ★ **Norseman Restaurant** (709/754-3105, late May-late Sept. daily noon-9pm, $19-36). Admittedly, the ocean views add to the appeal, but the food is fresh and creative, the service professional, and the setting casual yet refined. Starters include a smooth shellfishless seafood chowder, smoked char, and lots of salads. Ordering lobster takes a little more effort than usual—you'll be invited to wander across the road with your waitress to pick one from an ocean pound. Other entrées include cod baked in a mustard and garlic crust and grilled Labrador caribou brushed with a red-wine glaze. Still hungry? It's hard to go past a slice of freshly baked pie filled with local berries.

The ★ **Dark Tickle Company** (75 Main St., Griquet, 709/623-2354, June-Sept. daily 9am-6pm, Oct.-May Mon.-Fri. 9am-5pm) uses locally harvested berries to create a delicious array of jams, preserves, sauces, and even chocolates and wines. You can watch the various processes in creating the finished product, but you'll also want to sample and purchase them from the attached store.

Accommodations and Camping

The village of L'Anse aux Meadows comprises just a smattering of homes on the headland. For overnight accommodations, there are a few choices back toward St. Anthony, all more enjoyable than staying in one of St. Anthony's nondescript motels.

The closest accommodations are in Hay Cove, a cluster of houses two kilometers before the end of the road. Stay in one of four comfortable guest rooms at **Jenny's Runestone House** (709/623-2811 or 877/865-3958, www.jennysrunestonehouse.ca, Apr.-Oct., $90-150 s or d) and enjoy ocean views and a hot breakfast each morning. Also in Hay Cove, **Viking Village Bed and Breakfast** (709/623-2238 or 877/858-2238, www.vikingvillage.ca, $65 s, $88 d) has five en suite guest rooms, ocean views, a TV room, and laundry facilities.

The units at **Southwest Pond Cabins** (Rte. 436, Griquet, 709/623-2140 or 800/515-2261, www.southwestpondcabins.ca, May-Oct., $109 s or d), overlooking a small lake nine kilometers from L'Anse aux Meadows, are an excellent value. Each of 10 spacious wooden cabins has a kitchen, separate bedrooms, satellite TV, and a bathroom. Other amenities include a playground, barbecues, and a grocery store.

At the top of the list for originality is ★ **Quirpon Lighthouse Inn** (Quirpon Island, 709/634-2285 or 877/254-6586, www.linkumtours.com, May-Oct., $275-325 s, $375-425 d), a converted light-keeper's residence and modern addition that house a total of 11 guest rooms, each with an en suite bath. Rates include all meals and boat transfers (45 minutes) from Quirpon. To get to Quirpon, turn off Route 436, six kilometers beyond Griquet. Watch icebergs float by and whales frolic in the surrounding waters, or join a Zodiac tour searching out whales and icebergs ($50 extra pp).

One of the few commercial campgrounds this far north is **Viking RV Park** (Rte. 436, Quirpon, 709/623-2425, June-Sept.), where tent campers pay $18 and RVs wanting hook-ups are charged $28 per night.

Getting There

It's 40 kilometers (40 minutes) north from St. Anthony to L'Anse aux Meadows via Route 430 and Route 436. From the ferry terminal in Port-aux-Basques, it's 700 kilometers (10 hours) north to L'Anse aux Meadows via Route 1, 430, and 436.

RALEIGH

Between St. Anthony and L'Anse aux Meadows, Route 437 branches off Route 436 to the delightfully named Ha Ha Bay and the small town of Raleigh.

★ Burnt Cape Ecological Reserve

Encompassing a barren landscape of lime-stone, the **Burnt Cape Ecological Reserve** is an unheralded highlight of the Northern Peninsula. The plant life is especially nota-ble, as many species would normally only be found in Arctic regions, while others, such as Long's Braya and Burnt Cape cinquefoil, are found nowhere else in the world. A geologi-cal oddity are polygons, circular patterns of small stones formed by heavy frosts. On the western edge of the cape are sea caves, some big enough to hold pools of water when the tide recedes. Looking straight ahead from the parking lot, you'll see aquamarine pools of water at the base of the cliffs, known lo-cally as the Cannon Holes. The sun reflecting on the limestone bedrock warms the trapped seawater, and you'll often see locals taking a dip on hot days.

To get there, turn left in downtown Raleigh, round the head of Ha Ha Bay, and follow the rough unpaved road up and through the bar-rens. The end of the road is a semi-official parking lot high above the ocean, four kilo-meters from the interpretive board at the en-trance to the reserve. As there are no marked trails and many of the highlights are hid-den from view, stop by the office at **Pisolet Bay Provincial Park** (just before Raleigh, 709/454-7570) for directions and up-to-date information on access.

Accommodations and Camping

The only accommodation in town is a good one—**Burnt Cape Cabins** (709/452-3521, www.burntcape.com, $129-149 s or d), which is beside a **café** (daily 8am-9pm) serving inex-pensive seafood and lobster dinners. Each of the seven modern cabins has a TV, Internet ac-cess, and comfortable beds, or choose to rent the affiliated three-bedroom home ($189).

Just before Route 437 descends to Raleigh, it passes **Pisolet Bay Provincial Park** (709/454-7570, June-mid-Sept., $18), which offers 30 sites, a kitchen shelter, washrooms with showers, and a lake with a beach and swimming for the brave.

Getting There

To get to Raleigh from St. Anthony, it's 30 ki-lometers (25 minutes) north via Route 430 and Route 437. From the ferry terminal in Port-aux-Basques, it's 690 kilometers (10 hours) north to Raleigh via Route 1, Route 430, and Route 437.

Labrador

Labrador Straits 88

North Coast 98

Central Labrador. 94

Look for ★ to find recommended
sights, activities, dining, and lodging.

Highlights

★ **L'Anse Amour:** North America's oldest known burial site and an imposing stone lighthouse combine to make the short detour to the "cove of love" a highlight (page 89).

★ **Red Bay National Historic Site:** Four Spanish galleons lie in Red Bay; onshore displays tell their story and that of what was at one time the world's largest whaling port (page 91).

★ **Battle Harbour:** Known locally as "outports," dozens of remote communities throughout Newfoundland and Labrador have been abandoned over the last few decades. Battle Harbour is one of the few that encourages tourism (page 92).

★ **North West River:** A short drive from Happy Valley-Goose Bay, this small community is home to the Labrador Interpretation Centre, while down along the river you can watch local Innu hauling in the day's catch (page 94).

★ **Torngat Mountains National Park:** This remote park can only be reached by charter flight, but once there, adventurous visitors can explore the mountains on foot and the coastline by kayak (page 100).

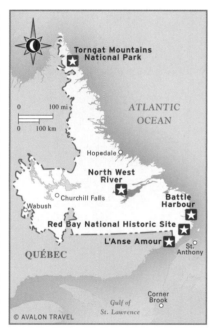

Spanning 294,330 square kilometers, two and a half times the size of Newfoundland island and three times the size of the three Maritime provinces, Labrador dominates the geography of Atlantic Canada.

This, the mainland portion of Newfoundland and Labrador, resembles an irregular wedge pointing toward the North Pole, bordered on the east by 8,000 kilometers of coastline on the Labrador Sea, and on the west and south by the remote outskirts of Québec. Thorfinn Karlsefni, one of several Norse explorers who sailed the coastline around AD 1000, is said to have dubbed the region "Helluland" for the large flat rocks, and "Markland" for the woodlands. Jacques Cartier described the coastline as a "land of stone and rocks" during a 1534 voyage.

Labrador can be divided into three geographical destinations. Along the Strait of Belle Isle—the narrow passage between Labrador and Newfoundland—is a string of communities fronting the strait. Known as the Labrador Straits and linked to Newfoundland by ferry, this region was a Basque whaling center in the 1500s. Modern sightseers have rediscovered the strait and its archaeological treasures at Red Bay and L'Anse Amour. Spruce forests, interspersed with bogs and birch and tamarack stands, dominate the wilderness of central Labrador. The watery complex of Lobstick Lake, Smallwood Reservoir, Michikamau Lake, and the Churchill River and its tributaries are the main geographical features. The Churchill flows out of the western saucer-shaped plateau and rushes eastward, widening into Lake Melville at the commercial hub of Happy Valley-Goose Bay, which grew from an important military base. In western Labrador, iron-ore mining developed in the late 1950s. The twin cities of Labrador City and Wabush started as mining towns, and together they now serve as the region's economic and transportation center. With a population of 11,300, Labrador City/Wabush is Labrador's largest municipality. Between Labrador City and Happy Valley-Goose Bay, a massive hydroelectric plant, developed in

---

Previous: kayaking along Labrador's North Coast; Battle Harbour. **Above:** Pinware River.

Labrador

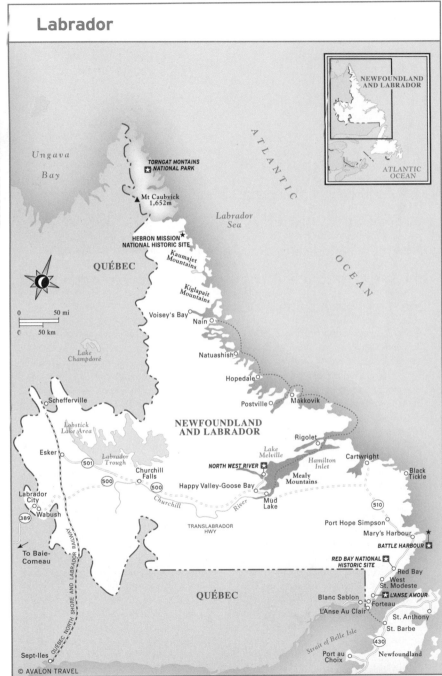

LABRADOR

NEWFOUNDLAND
AND LABRADOR

ATLANTIC
OCEAN

*Ungava
Bay*

ATLANTIC

TORNGAT MONTAINS
NATIONAL PARK

▲ Mt Caubvick
1,652m

*Labrador
Sea*

HEBRON MISSION
NATIONAL HISTORIC SITE

*Kaumajet
Mountains*

QUÉBEC

OCEAN

*Kiglapait
Mountains*

Voisey's Bay○

Nain ○

| 0 | 50 mi |
| 0 | 50 km |

*Lake
Champdoré*

Natuashish○

Hopedale○

Scheffervile○

Postville○   ○Makkovik

*Lobstick
Lake Area*

**NEWFOUNDLAND
AND LABRADOR**

Rigolet○

*Lake
Melville*

Esker○

*Labrador
Trough*

(501)

Churchill
Falls

(500)

(500)

NORTH WEST RIVER

*Hamilton
Inlet*

Cartwright
○

○Black
Tickle

Happy Valley-Goose Bay○

*Mealy
Mountains*

Labrador
City

○Wabush

(389)

Churchill   River

Mud
Lake

(510)

To Baie-
Comeau

TRANSLABRADOR
HWY

Port Hope Simpson○

Mary's Harbour○

BATTLE HARBOUR

**RED BAY NATIONAL
HISTORIC SITE**

Red Bay○
West
St. Modeste

QUÉBEC

Blanc Sablon○

L'ANSE AMOUR

L'Anse Au Clair○

○Forteau

○ St. Anthony

○ St. Barbe

QUÉBEC NORTH SHORE AND LABRADOR RAILWAY

Sept-Iles○

Strait of Belle Isle

Port au
Choix

(430)

Newfoundland

© AVALON TRAVEL

the late 1960s, spawned another company town—Churchill Falls. Linked to the outside world by ferry, the North Coast is dotted with tiny Inuit settlements within the Nunatsiavut land claim area.

Labrador is very popular with serious anglers, who rank the sportfishing here among the world's best. And the fishing is said to be Atlantic Canada's finest as well: It's not uncommon to land an *ouananiche* (landlocked salmon) weighing four kilograms. Brook trout here range 3-4 kilograms, lake trout to 18 kilograms, northern pike 9-14 kilograms, and arctic char 5-7 kilograms.

PLANNING YOUR TIME

Because of its remote location, Labrador is the least-visited region of Atlantic Canada. It can be divided into three regions—Labrador Straits, across the Strait of Belle Isle from Newfoundland's Northern Peninsula; Central Labrador, along the TransLabrador Highway; and the North Coast. While the northern regions attract serious adventurers, the main attractions lie along the Labrador Straits, easily accessible by ferry from the Northern Peninsula, where along a 120-kilometer stretch of highway is a string of picturesque fishing villages. Some are more

historic than others. At **L'Anse Amour,** you can view North America's oldest known burial site; **Red Bay National Historic Site** tells the story of a Basque whaling port. One of the most moving experiences in all of Atlantic Canada is a visit to **Battle Harbour,** an island fishing community that was abandoned in the late 1960s. Today you can relive the glory days of this remote port, and even stay overnight. Unlike many other destinations, getting to and traveling around Labrador is part of the adventure, and nothing is more "out there" than exploring the remote northern wilderness of **Torngat Mountains National Park.**

Getting around Labrador requires some advance planning. The communities of Labrador Straits are linked by Route 510 from Blanc Sablon, where ferries land from Newfoundland. The 510 extends north from Port Hope Simpson for 370 kilometers through Cartwright Junction to Happy Valley-Goose Bay. From Happy Valley-Goose Bay, it's 520 kilometers west to Labrador City.

Deciding *when* to travel to Labrador is easy. July and August are the only two months during which you'll find all attractions open. June and September are shoulder

hiking in Torngat Mountains National Park

months, when the weather is cooler and attractions begin opening and closing. Also be aware that transportation is conducted on a weather-permitting basis. Early-season ice packs and late-season storms can delay the ferries. The region's smaller aircraft need daylight and good visibility. An absence of both may ground flights for days.

Labrador Straits

The communities of Labrador Straits lie across the Strait of Belle Isle from Newfoundland. They are linked by a 160-kilometer stretch of paved road that extends between Blanc Sablon (Québec) and Mary's Harbour. From Mary's Harbour, an unpaved road loops inland and continues north to Goose Bay.

Getting There by Ferry

The ferry **MV Apollo** (866/535-2567, www.labradormarine.com, one-way vehicle and driver $36, extra adult $12, senior and child $10) links the Labrador Straits to Newfoundland. Ferries depart St. Barbe, 300 kilometers north of Deer Lake, once or twice daily early May-early January. The crossing takes around two hours. The arrival point is Blanc Sablon, located in Québec but just a five-minute drive from L'Anse-au-Clair, within Labrador. If the weather is pleasant, find a spot outside and keep an eye out for whales. Inside the ferry are a café and gift shop. Reservations are not required but are definitely recommended for travel in July and August. Even with a reservation, upon arrival at St. Barbe you should check in at the ferry office. It is within the Dockside Motel (on the right before the terminal) and opens two hours before scheduled departures. At Blanc Sablon, the ferry office is at the terminal, along with a craft shop, food concession, and information booth.

L'ANSE-AU-CLAIR

Founded in the early 18th century by French sealers, L'Anse-au-Clair is the closest strait community to the Québec border. Fishing is still the livelihood for the population of about 300, although crafts also contribute to the economy. For these, head to **Moore's Handicrafts** (8 Country Rd., 709/931-2086, June-Sept. daily 8:30am-9pm), signposted across from the information center. Pieces to look for include hand-knit woolens, winter coats, cassocks, and moccasins.

Sights and Recreation

The **Gateway to Labrador Visitor Centre** (38 Main Hwy., 709/931-2013, www.labradorcoastaldrive.com, mid-June-Sept. daily 9am-6pm), the region's interpretive center, seen as you enter town from Québec, is in a handsomely restored, early 20th-century Anglican church. Inside, exhibits, photographs, fossils, and artifacts represent the area's fishing heritage.

The information center staff can also point out two interesting walks. The shorter of the two is to the **"Jersey Rooms,"** site of an early-1700s sealing station operated by men from Jersey. Only stone foundations and a stone walkway remain, but the two-kilometer trail also offers sweeping ocean views. The trailhead is signposted beyond the wharf. At the far end of the beach, a trail leads across the barrens to **Square Cove,** where the boilers are all that remain of a 1954 shipwreck. In August, wild strawberries are a bonus along this three-kilometer (each way) walk.

Food and Accommodations

The largest accommodation along the Labrador Straits is the **Northern Light Inn** (58 Main St., 709/931-2332 or 800/563-3188, www.northernlightinn.com, $119-169 s or d), which has 70 comfortable rooms and a few RV sites ($28). The inn's **restaurant** (daily

ferry to the Labrador Straits

a light breakfast, cottage $165 s or d), in a nursing station built by the International Grenfell Association. The five guest rooms are comfortable but share bathrooms, or choose the adjacent two-bedroom cottage with full kitchen. Other amenities include an antiques-filled dining room and a lounge where you can watch films on the Grenfell legacy or read up on local history.

Along the highway in the center of town, **Seaview Restaurant and Cabins** (33 Main St., 709/931-2840 or 800/931-2840, www.labradorseaview.ca, $100-110 s or d) has motel rooms, not cabins, but they are comfortable, and each has one or two bedrooms, a kitchen, and wireless Internet. The **restaurant** (daily 11am-9pm, $12-24) has simple preparations of locally caught cod, char, and salmon.

Getting There

Forteau is 10 kilometers east of L'Anse au Clair via Route 510.

★ L'ANSE AMOUR

Just off Route 510, this tiny community comprises just four houses, all owned by members of the Davis family, residents since the 1850s. The bay was originally named Anse aux Morts ("Cove of the Dead") for the many shipwrecks that occurred in the treacherous waters offshore. A mistranslation by later English settlers resulted quite charmingly in the name **L'Anse Amour** ("Cove of Love").

Maritime Archaic Burial Mound National Historic Site

Turn off Route 510 to L'Anse Amour and watch for a small interpretive board on the right, which marks the **Maritime Archaic Burial Mound National Historic Site.** Here, in 1973, archaeologists uncovered a Maritime Archaic burial site of a 12-year-old boy dated to 6900 BC, which makes it North America's oldest known funeral monument. The dead boy was wrapped in skins and birch bark and placed face-down a pit. Items such as a walrus tusk were excavated from the pit, and

7am-10pm, $16-32) is well priced throughout the day, with dinner mains topping out at $32 for steamed crab legs with mashed potato and vegetables. Other dinner offerings are as simple as spaghetti and meatballs and as fishy as pan-fried cod.

FORTEAU

Established as a cod-fishing settlement by islanders from Jersey and Guernsey in the late 1700s, Forteau remains a fishing community, not only in the cod industry but also as a base for anglers fishing the salmon- and trout-filled Forteau and Pinware Rivers.

The **Bakeapple Folk Festival,** held over three days in mid-August, is always popular. The gathering includes traditional music, dance, storytelling, crafts, and Labrador foods.

Food and Accommodations

Forteau's accommodations include the **Grenfell Louie A Hall Bed and Breakfast** (3 Willow Ave., 709/931-2916, www.grenfellbandb.ca, May-Sept., $100 s, $110 d, including

The Grenfell Legend

Labrador's harsh living conditions and lack of medical care attracted Dr. Wilfred Grenfell, the British physician-missionary. Dr. Grenfell worked with the Royal National Mission to Deep Sea Fishermen on the North Sea. A visit in 1892 convinced him that serving the people of remote Labrador and northern Newfoundland was his calling. He established Labrador's first coastal hospital at Battle Harbour the next year, followed by a large mission at St. Anthony. From the mission, he sailed along the coast in boats, treating 15,000 patients in 1900 alone. By 1907 he had opened treatment centers at Indian Harbour, Forteau, North West River, and seven other remote settlements. For his efforts, he was knighted.

Dr. Grenfell initiated a policy of free medical treatment, clothing, or food in exchange for labor or goods. Funded by private contributions and the Newfoundland government, he opened cooperative stores, nursing homes, orphanages, mobile libraries, and lumber mills. He also initiated the Grenfell Handicrafts programs and home gardening projects. In 1912, he formed the International Grenfell Association to consolidate the English, Canadian, and American branches that funded his work. The physician was subsequently knighted a second time, in 1927, and also awarded recognition by the Royal Scottish Geographical Society and other notable organizations.

other evidence points to a ceremonial feast. The artifacts found here are on display at The Rooms in St. John's.

Point Amour Lighthouse

At the end of the road is **Point Amour Lighthouse** (709/927-5825, late May-early Oct. daily 9:30am-5pm, adult $6, senior $4, child $3). The strait's rich sea has attracted intrepid fishing fleets through the centuries: The early Basques sailed galleons into Red Bay, followed by English and French fleets, and eventually Newfoundlanders arrived in schooners to these shores. By 1857, shipwrecks littered the treacherous shoals, and the colonial government erected this 33-meter-high beacon, Atlantic Canada's tallest. Now restored, the stone lighthouse and light-keeper's residence (now the interpretive center) feature displays and exhibits on the history of those who have plied the strait's waters. The 122-step climb to the top

Point Amour Lighthouse

(the final section is a ladder) affords excellent views of the strait and the surrounding land.

Accommodations

One of the village's four homes operates as ★ **Lighthouse Cove B&B** (709/927-5690, $50 s, $60 d), with three rooms open year-round for travelers. The hosts, Rita and Cecil Davis, are very hospitable, spending the evening with guests relating stories of the area and their family's long association with the cove. When you make a reservation, be sure to reserve a spot at the dinner table (extra) for a full meal of traditional Labrador cooking, using game such as moose and caribou. Breakfast, included in the rate, comes with homemade preserves.

Getting There

L'Anse Amour is 12 kilometers east of Forteau on Route 510.

RED BAY

Little evidence is left today, but 400 years ago, Red Bay was the world's largest whaling port. Not discovered until the 1970s, four Spanish galleons at the bottom of the bay have taught archaeologists many secrets about the whaling industry and early boat construction; an excellent national historic site here brings the port to life. The village itself, 40 kilometers north of L'Anse Amour, has limited services.

It is estimated that between 1540 and 1610, around 2,500 Basque men (from an area of Spain near the French border) made the crossing from Europe each year, traveling in up to 30 galleons that returned to Europe filled with whale oil. The Basques came to harvest right whales, which migrated through the Strait of Belle Isle. Most of the men lived aboard the galleons, but evidence shows that some built simple shelters on the mainland and Saddle Island, where red roof tiles still litter the beaches.

★ Red Bay National Historic Site

Four Spanish galleons lie in Red Bay, including the well-preserved *San Juan*. Archaeologists have done extensive research on all four, and they now lie in the cold shallow water covered with tarpaulins. While you can't view the actual boats, two excellent facilities combine to make up **Red Bay National Historic Site** (709/920-2051, June-late Sept. daily 9am-5pm, adult $8, senior $6.50, child $4). Coming off the highway, the first of the two site buildings is a modern structure centering on a *chalupa*, another wooden whaling boat recovered from the bottom of Red Bay. You can watch a documentary on the galleon *San Juan* and have staff point out where each of the galleons is located. Keep your receipt and head toward the waterfront, where the main collection of artifacts is held. Displays describe how the four galleons, each from a different era, have helped archaeologists track ship design through the 16th and 17th centuries. Highlights include a scale model of the *San Juan*, pottery, and remains of a compass and sandglass.

Food and Accommodations

The single lodging choice at Red Bay is **Basin View B&B** (Rte. 510, 709/920-2002, $65-85 s or d, including a light breakfast), a modern home overlooking the bay from a rocky shoreline just before reaching the town itself. The three downstairs rooms share a single bathroom. The upstairs guest room has a private bathroom but less privacy, as it is on the main level of the house.

Down by the harbor but without water views, **Whaler's Station Restaurant** (72 W. Harbour Dr., 709/920-2156, daily 8am-9pm, $11-19) is one of the region's better dining rooms. The seafood chowder is good, as is the beef soup. For a main, the fish-and-chips is as good as it gets in Labrador, while the pork chop dinner is simple and hearty.

Getting There

Red Bay is 60 kilometers (one hour) north of L'Anse Amour via Route 510.

MARY'S HARBOUR

Beyond Red Bay, Route 510 is unpaved for 80 kilometers to Mary's Harbour. This small fishing village, where the local economy revolves around a crab-processing plant, was isolated until 2000, when the road was completed.

The main reason to travel this far north is to visit Battle Harbour, and since the ferry leaves from Mary's Harbour, the local **Riverlodge Hotel** (709/921-6948, www.riverlodgehotel.ca, $110-125 s or d) makes a sensible overnight stop. The 15 rooms are simple but comfortable (rates include wireless Internet), and the in-house restaurant has pleasant views across the St. Mary's River.

Getting There

Mary's Harbour is about 90 kilometers (one hour) north of Red Bay via Route 510.

★ BATTLE HARBOUR

On a small island an hour's boat ride from Mary's Harbour lies **Battle Harbour,** a remote yet intriguing outport village that is well worth the effort to reach.

Established as a fishing village in 1759, it was one of the earliest European settlements on the Labrador coast. By 1775, Battle Harbour's cod-fishing industry had made the settlement the economic center of the region, a status that faded and then rebounded a century later with the arrival of seasonal fishers from Newfoundland. By 1848 Battle Harbour was the capital of Labrador, an important trade and supply center where up to 100 vessels would be tied up in port at any one time. Thanks to the work of missionary Wilfred Grenfell, the residents had year-round medical services and, by 1904, state-of-the-art communications thanks to the Marconi Wireless Telegraph Company, which erected a station here in 1904.

In the late 1960s, with the inshore fishery in decline, Battle Harbour residents were resettled on the mainland at Mary's Harbour, leaving the community an abandoned outport. A few local families continued to spend summers on the island, but it wasn't until 1990 that the Battle Harbour Historic Trust took over the site and began an ambitious restoration program that continues to this day. Now protected as a national historic site, Battle Harbour allows a glimpse into the past. About 20 structures have been restored, including an Anglican church, the original mercantile salt fish premises, the loft from

Battle Harbour

which Robert Peary told the world of his successful expedition to reach the North Pole, a general store, and a massive fish "flake" (drying platform). A boardwalk links many of the restored buildings, tapering off near the back of the village, where a dozen or so homes stand in varying states of disrepair and a trail leads through a rock cleft to a cemetery.

Visiting Battle Harbour

In addition to restoring many of the most important buildings, the **Battle Harbour Historic Trust** (709/921-6325, www.battleharbour.com) does a wonderful job of providing visitor services, including accommodations, meals, and transportation, all of which are packaged together. Rates, inclusive of transportation to the island, meals, and accommodations, range from $250 per person for the first night (S155 for subsequent nights) for dormitory-style bunk beds to $545 for the first night ($355 for subsequent nights) in a private room in the Battle River Inn. On a rise overlooking the town and Great Caribou Island, the inn is a beautifully restored merchant's home where three of the five guest rooms have double beds; two have single beds. Other buildings with beds include the hostel-style Cookhouse; the Grenfell Doctor's Cottage, which has harbor views; the Constable Forward Cottage; the three-bedroom Isaac Smith Cottage, which is lighted by oil lamps and heated by wood fire; and the very private two-bedroom Spearing Cottage. Meals are provided in a dining room above the general store. All are hearty, with plenty of cross-table conversation between diners. At the general store itself, you can buy snacks and basic provisions.

Getting There and Around

The trip between Mary's Harbour and Battle Harbour takes around one hour aboard a small enclosed ferry (inn guests only). The ferry departs Mary's Harbour in the summer daily at 11am, and the return trip departs Battle Harbour at 9am. The ferry transfer is included in all overnight packages. Once on the island, all lodging is within easy walking distance of the ferry dock.

CARTWRIGHT

Most travelers incorporate Cartwright into their itineraries as part of a loop that includes driving the TransLabrador Highway through to Happy Valley-Goose Bay.

From Mary's Harbour, it is 157 kilometers to Cartwright Junction (no services), from where the TransLabrador Highway continues around the Mealy Mountains to Happy Valley-Goose Bay; Cartwright is 87 kilometers north along Route 516

Sights

The town was named for 18th-century merchant adventurer and coastal resident Captain George Cartwright; **Flagstaff Hill Monument,** overlooking the town and Sandwich Bay, still has the cannons Cartwright installed to guard the harbor 200 years ago.

Gannet Islands Ecological Reserve, off the coast, is a breeding colony for common murres, puffins, black-legged kittiwakes, and the province's largest razorbill population. North of Cartwright lies the spot where Norse sailors first laid eyes on the coast: **Wunderstrands,** a magnificent 56-kilometer stretch of sandy golden beach across Sandwich Bay that is only accessible by boat. The local tour operator, **Experience Labrador** (709/653-2244 or 877/938-7444, www.experiencelabrador.com), offers sea kayaking day trips, but you're missing the local highlight if you simply paddle around local waterways and don't take a day trip to the Wunderstrand. Now protected as part of Mealy Mountains National Park, the beach was named by infamous Viking Erik the Red and to this day receives few visitors. The cost is $250 s, $300 d for the six-hour adventure, booked through Experience Labrador.

Food and Accommodations

The centrally located **Northside Motel** (14 Low Rd., 709/938-7577, $95 s, $105 d) is a simple six-room affair, with a friendly little pub attached to the back.

Getting There

Cartwright is about 250 kilometers (3.5 hours) north of Mary's Harbour via Route 530 and Route 516.

Central Labrador

HAPPY VALLEY-GOOSE BAY

Happy Valley-Goose Bay (pop. 7,550) spreads across a sandy peninsula bordered by the Churchill River, Goose Bay, and Terrington Basin at the head of Lake Melville. Although remote, it is linked to the outside world by the TransLabrador Highway (Churchill Falls is 288 kilometers to the west, and Blanc Sablon is 620 kilometers southeast) and scheduled air services.

During World War II, Canadian forces selected the Goose Bay site and, with assistance from the British Air Ministry and the U.S. Air Force, built a massive airbase and two airstrips there. Before the war ended, 24,000 aircraft set down for refueling during the transatlantic crossing. Currently operated by the Canadian Armed Forces, 5 Wing Goose Bay Airport serves as a training center for Canadian, British, Dutch, Italian, and German air forces, since the latter four countries have no airspace of their own suitable for low-level flight training. Goose Bay is also an important refueling stop for transatlantic flights, with a runway long enough to accommodate space shuttle landings in an emergency. The town last hit the headlines on September 11, 2001, when the airport filled with commercial flights that were diverted from their intended destinations.

Happy Valley-Goose Bay originally evolved as two distinct areas: Goose Bay, rimming an important air base, and adjacent Happy Valley, which became the base's residential and commercial sector. In 1961 the two areas joined as Happy Valley-Goose Bay and elected the first town council, which was Labrador's first municipal government. The distinction between the two areas remains firm, so be prepared to consult a map as you wander around. Goose Bay connects to Happy Valley by the L-shaped Hamilton River Road, the main drag.

Town Sights

In the Northern Lights Building, the **Northern Lights Military Museum** (170 Hamilton River Rd., 709/896-5939, Tues.-Sat. 9am-5:30pm, free) offers exhibits pertaining to military history from World War I to the Vietnam War. Displays include uniforms, medals, documents, weapons, and photographs. Across the hall, the **Trapper's Brook Animal Display** exhibits stuffed native animals and birds—from beavers and bears to bald eagles. At the **Labrador Institute** (219 Hamilton River Rd., 709/896-6210, call for hours), an arm of Memorial University of Newfoundland, there are often Labrador-oriented artifacts on display, as well as an archive of historical maps and photographs open to the public.

★ North West River

This community of 500, 38 kilometers northeast of Goose Bay on Route 520, was the center of the area until the 1940s. The settlement began as a French trading post in 1743, and the inhabitants are descendants of French, English, and Scottish settlers.

Within town are two worthwhile sights. The **Labrador Interpretation Centre** (2 Portage Rd., 709/497-8566, early May-Sept. Mon.-Sat. 9am-4:30pm, Sun. noon-4:30pm, free) is filled with interesting exhibits that

Happy Valley-Goose Bay

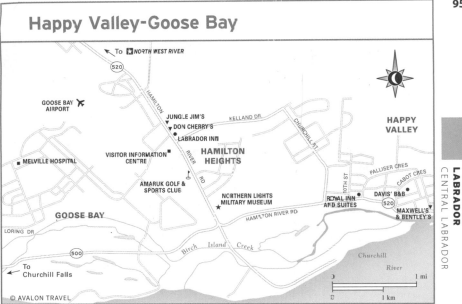

catalog the natural and human history of "the Big Land." Beyond the center, Portage Road leads to piers and pleasant views. If you'd like to meet some of the locals, arrive in late afternoon, when the Innu fishers collect the day's catch from nets strung across the waterway. Within an original Hudson's Bay Company building, the **Labrador Heritage Museum** (Portage Rd., 709/497-8858, July-Aug. daily 8:30am-4:30pm, adult $2, child $1) provides an insight into Labrador's early years with photographs, manuscripts, books, artifacts, furs, native minerals, and other displays.

Food

Fast-food places line Hamilton River Road, including the ubiquitous and ever-popular **Tim Hortons** (220 Hamilton River Rd., 709/896-5666, open 24 hours), a coffee-and-donut chain beloved by Canadians.

The casual **Jungle Jim's** (Hotel North Two, 382 Hamilton River Rd., 709/896-3398, daily 11am-2am, $14-27) features a menu of typical Canadian dishes. Next door in the Labrador Inn, **Don Cherry's** (380 Hamilton River Rd., 709/896-3351, daily 7am-2pm and 5pm-10pm, $16-29) is a sports bar with an extensive menu of standard pub fare at prices that are probably a bit higher than you want to pay.

The closest thing to a splurge in all of Labrador would be dinner at **Maxwell's and Bentley's** (97 Hamilton River Rd., 709/896-3565, Mon.-Sat. 11am-9:30pm, $12-27), which combines a restaurant (Bentley's) with a nightclub (Maxwell's). The restaurant section is a semi-stylish, air-conditioned room overlooking the Churchill River. The food is fairly predictable, with the usual array of steak, chicken, pork, and seafood dishes.

Accommodations

B&Bs offer the least-expensive lodgings. **Davis' Bed and Breakfast** (14 Cabot Cres., Happy Valley. 709/896-5077, $60-80 s, $80-100 d) has four guest rooms with private baths and wireless Internet. Rates include a continental breakfast (a full breakfast costs extra). Facilities include a dining room, laundry, and an outside patio.

Happy Valley-Goose Bay has several motels catering mostly to business travelers. In general, rooms are of an acceptable standard and expensive, but not outrageously so. The **Royal Inn and Suites** (3 Royal Ave., Goose Bay, 709/896-2456 or 888/440-2456, www.royalinnandsuites.ca, $120-170 s, $130-170 d) is my pick of the bunch. It has 35 guest rooms, including a few with separate bedrooms, TV/DVD combos, and kitchens.

Rooms at the **Labrador Inn** (380 Hamilton River Rd., 709/896-3351 or 800/563-2763, www.labradorinn.nf.ca, $120-160) are of a similar standard. Facilities here include a restaurant, a lounge, and airport shuttles.

Information and Services

Destination Labrador (709/896-6507, www.destinationlabrador.com) operates a helpful information center along the main drag (365 Hamilton River Rd., June-Sept. Mon.-Fri. 8am-8pm, Sat.-Sun. 8am-5pm).

Melville Hospital (also called Grenfell Hospital) is at Building 550, G Street (near 5th Avenue). For the **RCMP** (149 Hamilton River Rd.), call 709/896-3383. **Post offices** are located on Hamilton River Road and at the airport.

Getting There and Around

In 2010, the final link in the **TransLabrador Highway** was completed, and Goose Bay was linked to the rest of the province by road. The highway leading west to Churchill Falls (288 kilometers) was already in place, but the section leading south to the Labrador Straits was a much bigger undertaking for engineers (620 km to Blanc Sablon). To this day, much of the road is still unpaved and the going can be extremely slow, especially in spring before graders have completed their work. But if you're up for an adventure, the journey along one of North America's newest and most remote highways is well worth considering.

Air Canada (888/247-2262) flies into **Goose Bay Airport** (YYR, www.goosebayairport.com) from Halifax and Toronto. **Air Labrador** (709/758-0002 or 800/563-3042, www.airlabrador.com) flies between Goose Bay and St. Anthony on Newfoundland's Northern Peninsula. **Provincial Airlines** (709/576-3943 or 800/563-2800, www.provincialairlines.ca) has flights to Goose Bay from as far away as Montreal and St. John's.

Budget (709/896-2976) and **National** (709/896-5575) have rental cars in town and out at the airport, but neither company allows its vehicles on the TransLabrador Highway. **Cooney's Taxi** (709/896-3311) charges around $10 per trip anywhere within Goose Bay, and $20 between the airport and Happy Valley.

CHURCHILL FALLS

Churchill Falls (population 650), 288 kilometers west of Goose Bay, is a relatively modern town constructed to serve the needs of workers at the world's second-largest underground hydroelectric power station. The waters of the Churchill River drop more than 300 meters over a 32-kilometer section—ideal for generating hydroelectric power. In an incredible feat of engineering, the water is diverted underground to the massive generators, which produce 5,220 megawatts of electricity.

The 21-room **Midway Travel Inn** (709/925-3211 or 800/229-3269, www.midwaylabrador.ca, $165 s or d) is a modern lodging attached to a **restaurant** (daily 7am-10pm) and the main town office complex. Rates include use of an indoor pool, wireless Internet, and airport shuttles.

Getting There

To drive to Churchill Falls from Goose Bay, it's 288 kilometers (four hours) west via Route 500.

LABRADOR CITY AND WABUSH

Continuing west from Churchill Falls, the twin towns of Labrador City and Wabush, five kilometers apart, lie about 530 kilometers from Goose Bay and just 23 kilometers from the Québec-Labrador border. Labradorians knew of the area's iron-ore potential by the late 1800s, and massive ore deposits were

Laying Claim to Labrador

For centuries the French Canadians have asserted, "Labrador is part of Québec." And the British and the Newfoundlanders have traditionally countered, "Never!"

Labrador is a choice piece of property, and Québec has been a longtime avid suitor of North America's northeastern edge. Québec's interest in Labrador dates to 1744, when the French cut a deal with the British: Québec got jurisdiction over Labrador, but the island of Newfoundland got fishing rights in Labrador's coastal waters. The Treaty of Paris of 1763 went one step further, however, and awarded all of Labrador (not defined by a precise border) to Newfoundland. Newfoundland's claim gained more substance in 1825, when the British North America Act set Labrador's southern border with Québec at the 52nd parallel.

In the 1860s, when the Dominion of Canada was formed, the dispute over Labrador, formerly between France and England, now involved the new Confederation of Canada. Québec never disputed England's sovereignty over Labrador, but instead continued to question the location of the border. In 1898 the Québec border was unofficially as far east as what is now the town of Happy Valley-Goose Bay.

FOR SALE: LABRADOR

Newfoundland put Labrador up for sale in 1909 for $9 million, but there were no takers. In the ensuing years, Labrador's precise border became a tedious issue for England, and so in 1927 a judicial committee in London set Labrador's border at the "height of the land," the watershed line separating the Atlantic Ocean from Ungava Bay, the current provincial border of today. In the decision, Labrador acquired the wedge-shaped "Labrador Trough," a delta area rich in iron ore deposits and rivers perfect for harnessing hydroelectric power.

QUÉBEC'S CLOUT EMERGES

The only road access to Labrador is through Québec, so it is no surprise that that province became a major player in Labrador's economy. Québec bought into Labrador's hydroelectric fortune in the early 1970s. Québec's provincial Hydro-Québec now earns $200 million annually from within Labrador, while Newfoundland, another company shareholder, earns $12 million. Ironically, Newfoundland and Labrador receive none of the energy.

To this day, the province's western border remains to be fully surveyed, and Québec does not consider the issue settled. A fragile status quo exists between the two provinces, but the renaming of Newfoundland to Newfoundland and Labrador in 2001 brought official recognition to Labrador as part of Newfoundland.

NUNATSIAVUT

In 2004, Labrador's Inuit people were successful in a land-claim process that took 30 years to come to fruition. Led by the **Labrador Inuit Association** (709/922-2942, www.nunatsiavut. com), the indigenous people now have special rights to 142,000 square kilometers of land that extend north from Lake Melville to Torngat Mountains National Park. The latter was established as part of the claim.

discovered in 1958. The Iron Ore Company of Canada and Wabush Mines, served by the two towns, together rank as the Canadian steel industry's largest supplier. The two extract 20 million metric tons of iron ore a year.

Lodging in the two towns is limited to just over 100 rooms in three motels. The **Wabush Hotel** (9 Grenfell Dr., Wabush, 709/282-3221, www.wabushhotel.com, $125 s, $135 d) is an imposing property dating to the 1960s. The 68 rooms have been revamped a few times since, and services include two restaurants, including one serving a Chinese/Canadian buffet lunch and dinner. **Two Seasons Inn** (96 Avalon Dr., Labrador City, 709/944-2661 or 800/670-7667, www.twoseasonsinn.

ca, $140 s, $155 d) has the best 54 guest rooms in Labrador, airport shuttle service, a **restaurant** (6:30am-10pm daily), and a small fitness room.

At **Duley Lake Family Park** (10 km west of Labrador City, 709/282-3660, late May-Sept., $20), choose between campsites on either the lake or river. The campground has a sandy beach, boating, fishing, and picnicking. **Grande Hermine Park** (45 km east of Labrador City, 709/282-5369, June-Aug., $20) offers 45 powered sites and 30 unserviced sites. Facilities include a boat launch, a convenience store, and pedal boat rentals.

Getting There

From Churchill Falls to Labrador City and Wabush, it's a 240-kilometer (3.5-hour) drive west on Route 500.

North Coast

Labrador's northern coast evokes images of another world. It's the Labrador you might imagine: raw and majestic, with the craggy mountain ranges of Torngat, Kaumajet, and Kiglapait rising to the north.

The 1763 Treaty of Paris ceded the Labrador coastline to Britain's Newfoundland colony, but the imprint of European architecture only reached the northern seacoast when the Moravians, an evangelical Protestant sect from Bohemia, established mission stations with prefabricated wooden buildings in the early 19th century. It is in these remote north coast villages—Rigolet, Postville, Makkovik, and Nain—that the original inhabitants, the Inuit, have settled. Few aspects of these towns have changed over the last century, and the lifestyle of northern peoples here remains traditional.

Getting There

Access to Labrador's north coast is by air or sea. The communities are linked to the outside world by **Air Labrador** (709/753-5593 or 800/563-3042, www.airlabrador.com) from Goose Bay, or by a cargo and passenger ferry that takes two days to reach its northern turnaround point, Nain. Riding the ferry, the **MV *Northern Ranger,*** is a real adventure. The one-way fare for an adult between Goose Bay and Nain is $185. A single berth in a shared cabin costs $90, while a private cabin costs $320-650 s or d. For more information, call 800/563-6353. The website www.labradorferry.ca lists a schedule and prices.

MAKKOVIK

After stopping at Rigolet, the MV *Northern Ranger* starts its long haul through open ocean, reaching Makkovik (pop. 400) 18 hours after leaving Goose Bay. The ferry makes a 90-minute stop on the way north and a three-hour stop on the return journey. Makkovik was first settled in the early 1800s by a Norwegian fur trader; the Moravians constructed a mission here in 1896. Today this two-story building holds the **White Elephant Museum** (709/923-2425, July-Aug. daily 1pm-5pm, or by appointment). Local shops such as the **Makkovik Craft Centre** (709/923-2221, call for hours) sell Inuit crafts, including fur caps, boots and mittens, parkas, moose-hide moccasins, and bone and antler jewelry.

Right on the water, the **Adlavik Inn** (7 Willow Creek Ln., 709/923-2389, www.labradorabletours.com, $120 s, $150 d) has the only five guest rooms in town, so call ahead if your itinerary includes an overnight stay in Makkovik. Rooms have TVs and phones, and meals are served in an adjacent dining room.

HOPEDALE

About 110 nautical miles north of Makkovik and 122 miles short of Nain, the MV *Northern Ranger* makes a two-hour stop at Hopedale, just enough time to go ashore and visit the 1782 **Hopedale Mission National Historic Site** (709/933-3864, adult $5), containing the oldest wooden frame building east of Québec. Here, a restored Hudson's Bay Company storeroom has been converted into a museum; other site highlights include huts, a residence, and a graveyard. It generally opens whenever the ferry is in town.

Accommodations are provided at **Amaguk Inn** (3 Harbour Dr., 709/933-3750, www.amagukinn.ca), which charges $159-209 s or d for its 18 rooms. Meals are available at the inn for both guests and nonguests.

NAIN AND THE FAR NORTH

With stunning coastal scenery, stops at remote villages, and the chance to see whales and icebergs, the long trip north aboard the MV *Northern Ranger* ferry is a real adventure, but after two days on board, the captain's announcement of imminent arrival in Nain, administrative capital of Nunatsiavut, is welcome. In the early 1900s, an epidemic of Spanish flu—introduced from a supply ship—destroyed a third of the indigenous population on the northern coast. The Inuit who survived re-settled at Nain, which now has a population of just over 1,000 and is the northernmost municipality on the Labrador coast. Life is rugged this far north—electricity is provided by diesel generator; fuel and wood are used for domestic heat; local transportation is by boat in the summer and snowmobile in the winter. The only roads are within the town itself.

Food and Accommodations

For an overnight stay, there's just one option, the **Atsanik Lodge** (Sand Banks Rd., 709/922-2910, $155 s, $165 d). Each of the 25 rooms has cable TV, a phone, and a private bathroom. The lodge also has a lounge, restaurant, and laundry. Other town services include a couple of grocery stores, a post office, and a takeout food joint.

Getting There

If you've arrived on the ferry, you'll have just three hours ashore to explore the town before the return journey. The alternative is to

The MV *Northern Ranger* serves communities along the North Coast.

take the ferry one way and an **Air Labrador** (709/753-5593 or 800/563-3042) flight the other. The one-way fare to Goose Bay is around $520.

Voisey's Bay

Prior to the cod-fishing moratorium, the fishing industry dominated Labrador's Far North Coast, but now mining at Voisey Bay, 35 kilometers south, appears to be the economic engine of the future. It is home to world's largest known deposit of nickel and copper. The main processing facility was completed in early 2006, and now around 6,000 tons of nickel and copper concentrate are mined daily by over 400 workers, who live in temporary accommodations on-site.

Hebron Mission National Historic Site

Labrador's northernmost remaining Moravian mission is protected at **Hebron Mission National Historic Site,** on the shores of remote Kangershutsoak Bay, 140 nautical miles north of Nain. Building began on the mission complex, including a church, residence, and store, in 1829. The mission remained in operation until 1959. **Nature Trek Canada** (250/653-4265, www.

naturetrek.ca) can make a stop here on its custom guided tours along the northern Labrador coastline.

★ Torngat Mountains National Park

Established in 2006 as part of the Nunatsiavut land claim, the remote wilderness of **Torngat Mountains National Park** protects 9,700 square kilometers of the remote coastline and rugged Torngat Mountains at the northern tip of Labrador. Glaciation dominates the park's geology; its mountains are separated by deep fiords and lakes that have been carved by retreating glaciers, many of which are still present in pockets scattered through the park. The entire park is above the tree line, so instead of trees, its valleys are carpeted in a variety of tundra vegetation, including wildflowers, which carpet large expanses during the very short summer season. Huge herds of caribou migrate across the park's interior, while polar bears are common along the coast.

Unless you are a long-distance kayaker, the only way to reach the park is by charter flight from Goose Bay to Saglek and then a boat transfer into the park. Flights and all ground services are arranged by

Torngat Mountains National Park

The Torngats (855/867-6428, www.the-torngats.com). Owned by a branch of the Nunatsiavut government, and with a season extending mid-July-early September, this company's on-site camp is at the south end of the park. Although used mostly by park staff and researchers, the facility also offers a variety of services for park visitors. Expect to pay around $4,000 for flights from Happy Valley-Goose Bay, the boat transfer, tent accommodations for four nights, meals, and limited guiding.

The main **park office** (709/922-1290, Mon.-Fri. 9am-4:30pm) is in Nain, although the best source of information for planning your trip is www.pc.gc.ca/torngat, where you can download a visitors' guide and hiking maps.

Torngats Mountains Peak

Background

The Landscape 103

Plants and Animals 105

History 110

Government and Economy 116

People and Culture 118

The Landscape

Atlantic Canada forms one-twentieth of the country's total area. The provinces, and the distances separating them, are far larger than they may seem at first glance, compared against the vastness of the whole of Canada.

In the Beginning

Six hundred million years ago, the collision of the North American and European continental plates pushed up the Appalachian Mountains. The range's ribs, starting far to the south in Alabama, extend through New England and the Maritime provinces to the Gaspé Peninsula, whose highlands spread as far as Newfoundland. Geologists believe that the range was originally taller and more rugged than the modern Rockies. Glaciation and eons of erosion, however, have ground down the once-mammoth summits. The highest peak in the Atlantic provinces, northern Labrador's desolate Mount Caubvick, rises 1,729 meters above the Labrador Sea. Otherwise, great swaths of the region's terrain are mostly low and undulating, dipping and swelling in innumerable variations.

One of the reasons for this: glacial ice, uncountable trillions of tons of it, formed over the last four ice ages. Glaciers up to an estimated three kilometers thick weighed down on the elastic bedrock as recently as 14,000 years ago, submerging the coasts and counteracting the inexorable thrust of tectonic uplift. Some 350 million years ago, as the tectonic plates shifted, a great slab of the earth's crust slumped, forming the valley that would be flooded by a rising sea to form the Bay of Fundy only 6,000 years ago.

A Watery Wonderland

More than any other region of Canada, the Atlantic provinces are defined by water, which divides as well as unifies them. The Cabot Strait separates Nova Scotia's Cape Breton and the island of Newfoundland's southern coastline. Along Labrador's coast, currents from the chilly Labrador Sea move southward and fork into a channel known as the Strait of Belle Isle, which separates the island of Newfoundland from the mainland, while the rest of the current washes along Newfoundland's eastern coast.

The sea's pervasive presence is felt throughout the region, but the ties to the ocean are perhaps strongest Newfoundland, whose outer coasts confront the open Atlantic. The waters off Newfoundland in particular—the Gulf of St. Lawrence and the Grand Banks along the continental shelf—are among the most productive fisheries in the world, for five centuries an unbelievably rich resource for tuna, mackerel, herring, lobster, and cod.

CLIMATE

As a rule, though, extremes are moderated by proximity to the sea. The months from June through September are generally the most pleasant and popular for visiting. The regions' landscapes and seascapes are recast by the changing seasons. In springtime, occasional banks of thick fog blanket the coast from Yarmouth to St. John's. In summer, a pervasive balminess ripens Newfoundland's Codroy Valley. Autumn brings the last burst of Indian summer, coloring the forests until winter's sea winds swirl in and send the leaves tumbling away to finish another year.

The climate is harsher and more extreme in Newfoundland and Labrador than in the rest of Atlantic Canada. A sultry summer day can be interspersed with chilly breezes, brilliant sun, dark clouds, and showers from light to drenching. The island's eastern and southern seacoasts are often foggy because of the off-shore melding of the warm Gulf Stream and the cold Labrador current.

Overall, the island has cool, moist weather. Summer days average 16-21°C (60-70°F), dropping to 9-12°C (48-54°F) at night, but hot spells are common, and the swimming season starts by late June. The island's low-lying interior and coastal areas are warmest and sunniest. Annual rainfall averages 105 centimeters. Frost begins by early October on the southern coast, and earlier farther north. Snowfall averages 300 centimeters a year.

Winter high temperatures average -4°C (39°F) to 0°C (32°F), warm enough to turn snow to rain, while nighttime lows can tumble to -15°C (5°F). Expect year-round blustery winds along Marine Drive and nearby Cape Spear.

Labrador's climate is continental and subject to great extremes. Summers are short, cool to sometimes hot, and brilliantly sunny with periodic showers. A July day averages 21°C (70°F), but temperatures have been known to rise to 38°C (100°F) at Happy Valley-Goose Bay. Temperatures drop rapidly after mid-August. By November, daytime highs at Happy Valley-Goose Bay fall to 0°C (32°F). Winter is very cold and dry. Daytime high temperatures average -20°C (-4°F) in the subarctic, -18°C (0°F) to -21°C (-6°F) in the interior, and -51°C (-60°F) in the western area.

ENVIRONMENTAL ISSUES

The northeastern Atlantic fisheries have been the economic engine driving exploration and development of these coasts for centuries. In days past, codfish were said to carpet the sea floor of the shallow Grand Banks, and those who caught them—first with lines from small dories, then with nets, and finally from great trawlers that scour the sea—have hauled in untold millions of tons of not only cod but also flounder, salmon, pollack, haddock, anchovies, and dozens of other species. Today the fish are in serious trouble and so too, inexorably, are the people and communities whose lives have revolved around them.

Today, the state of local fisheries—most notably the collapse of cod stocks—is the most important environmental issue facing the region. The beginning of the end was the arrival of "factory ships" in the 1960s, which could harvest up to 200 tons of cod per hour. By the late 1980s, the cod stock had been

Some of the world's oldest rock is in Labrador and Newfoundland.

mostly obliterated, and by the early 1990s, a moratorium was put in place until the fisheries had recovered. Unfortunately, what was not fully understood at that time was that overfishing was only a part of the problem. Cod are a groundfish, and the factory ships had been bottom trawling—scooping up the cod in nets with an opening up to one kilometer wide that dragged along the sea floor and decimated the very ecosystem that was a breeding ground for the fish. It is widely thought that the cod stock will never fully recover, especially in the waters around the island of Newfoundland.

Plants and Animals

To a great extent, it was the land's natural resources—and the potential riches they represented—that attracted Europeans to Canada over the centuries. Since time immemorial, mammals, fish, and varied plant species had, of course, fed and clothed the indigenous peoples, who harvested only enough to sustain themselves. But the very abundance of the wildlife seemed to fuel the rapacity of the newcomers, driving them to a sort of madness of consumption—and hastening the exploration and settlement of the newfound continent.

Cod, flounder, mackerel, herring, and scores of other fish species in unbelievable numbers first lured brave seafarers across the Atlantic as early as the 15th century. The great whales, too, fell victim to widespread slaughter. Later, the fur-bearing mammals—mink, otters, ermines, beavers, and seals—became a currency of trade and the sine qua non of fashionable attire. Birds, too, by the millions in hundreds of species, represented money on the wing to the newcomers. Some, like the flightless great auk of the northeastern coast, were hunted to extinction.

But much remains, in sometimes astonishing abundance and variety, thanks to each species' own unique genius for survival, blind luck, the shifting vagaries of public tastes, and even the occasional glimmer of human enlightenment.

PLANTS

The receding glaciers of the last ice age scoured the land and left lifeless mud and rubble in their wake. Overall, the climate then was considerably cooler than it is today, and the first life forms to recolonize in the shadow of the glaciers were hardy mosses, lichens, and other cold-tolerant plants. Junipers and other shrubs later took root, and afterward came coniferous trees—hardy fast-growing spruce and fir—that could thrive here despite the harsh climate and relatively brief growing season. In the boggy interiors sprouted moisture-loving willows and tamaracks. As the climate warmed and the soil grew richer, broadleaf deciduous trees arrived, filling in the outlines of the forests still seen and enjoyed today.

Forests

Newfoundland's forests are dominated by black spruce and balsam fir, with occasional stands of larch, pin cherry, pine, paper and white birch, aspen, red and mountain maple, and alder. In Newfoundland's alpine and coastal areas, you may encounter the formidable "tuckamore," a thicket composed of stunted, hopelessly entangled fir and spruce. Labrador's southern forests are cloaked with spruce, tamarack, juniper, and birch. White spruce 30 meters tall dominate the central area, while stunted black spruce, a mere meter tall, form a stubble along the timberline area. Farther north on the arctic tundra, dwarf birch and willow are common.

Wildflowers and Other Plants

Trees, of course, are only part of the picture. Along the forest margins, raspberry and blackberry thickets proliferate, providing, among other benefits, welcome snacks for summertime hikers.

Across Newfoundland's marshes and bogs, you'll see white and yellow water lilies, rare orchid species, purple iris and goodwithy, and insectivorous plants (such as the pitcher plant, the provincial flower). Daisies, blue harebells, yellow goldenrod, pink wild roses, and deep pink fireweed thrive in the woodlands. Marsh marigolds, as bright yellow as daffodils, are native to the western coast's Port au Port Peninsula. Low dense mats of crowberry are common throughout Newfoundland and Labrador. The late-autumn crop of blue-black fruits is a favorite food of curlews, plovers, and other migrants preparing for their long flights to the Caribbean and South America. Yellow poppies, heather buttercups, miniature purple rhododendrons, violets, and deep blue gentian, mixed among the white cotton grass, brighten Labrador's arctic tundra; farther south, the daisy-like arnica and purple saxifrage grow in plateau-rock niches.

You may encounter poison ivy. Mushrooms are everywhere; be absolutely certain you know the species before sampling—the chanterelles are culinary prizes, but the amanitas deadly poison.

Along the Shore

Near the coasts, familiar plants—spruces, hardy cinnamon ferns, northern juniper—take on a stunted, gnarled look from contending with the unmitigated elements. It can take endurance and adaptation to survive here amid often harsh conditions. Trees and bushes lie cropped close to the ground or lean permanently swept back by the wind as if with a giant hairbrush.

Plants on or near the beach require specialization, too. Marram grass, also called American beach grass, is abundant all along the Atlantic coast. Its extensive root systems stabilize the sand dunes on which it grows. Another important dune plant, the beach heather, grows in low mats that trap sand and help keep the dunes in place. Small, abundant yellow flowers color large patches from May to July. Beach pea, seaside goldenrod, dusty miller, and sea rocket are a few of the other plants that can manage on the less-than-fertile soils just above the high-tide line. Lower down grow cord grass and glasswort, whose systems can tolerate regular soakings of saltwater.

Within the intertidal zone, there's a different world altogether amidst the surging seawater and tide pools. The great disparities between high and low tides help to make the rocky coasts of the Maritimes among the richest and most varied in the world. Low tide exposes thick mats of tough rubbery rockweed, or sea wrack, for a few hours each day. Farther out (or deeper down) is the lower intertidal zone of coral-pink to reddish-brown Irish moss and brilliant green sea lettuce, which carpet the rocks and harbor populations of starfish, crabs, and sea urchins.

The deepest stratum of plant life is what marine biologists call the laminarian zone, typified by giant brown kelps, such as the common horsetail kelp. These algae attach to rocks at depths up to 40 meters and grow rapidly toward the surface, their broad leathery fans and air bladders lilting with the rise and fall of the swells. Storms can prune the upper extremities or tear entire plants from their moorings to wash ashore along with the populations of tiny mollusks, crustaceans, and other creatures that made their homes among the fronds.

LAND MAMMALS

About 70 different land mammals call Atlantic Canada home. The ones you're most likely to come across are moose, deer, black bears, and beavers.

Moose

The giant of the deer family is the moose, an awkward-looking mammal that appears to have been designed by a cartoonist. It has the largest antlers of any animal in the world,

Caution: Moose on the Loose

Some locals won't drive on rural roads between dusk and dawn. The reason? Moose on the loose.

About 400 moose-and-car collisions occur annually in Newfoundland alone, where the moose population is 150,000 and growing. A moose collision is no mere fender-bender. These animals are big and heavy, and hitting one at speed will make a real mess of your car (it doesn't do the unfortunate moose much good either). Consequences can be fatal to both parties.

Seventy percent of collisions occur between May and October. Accidents occur mainly 11pm-4am (but that's no guarantee collisions won't happen at any hour). If you must drive after dark in areas frequented by moose, use the high beams, scan the sides of the road, and proceed with caution.

Provincial governments post signs marked with the figure of a moose along the most dangerous stretches of highway.

stands up to 1.8 meters tall at the shoulder, and weighs up to 500 kilograms. Its body is dark brown, and it has a prominent nose, long spindly legs, small eyes, big ears, and an odd flap of skin called a bell dangling beneath its chin. Each spring the bull begins to grow palm-shaped antlers that by August will be fully grown. Moose are solitary animals that prefer marshy areas and weedy lakes, but they are known to wander to higher elevations searching out open spaces in summer. They forage in and around ponds on willows, aspen, birch, grasses, and all aquatic vegetation. Although they may appear docile, moose will attack humans if they feel threatened.

Moose are most commonly found in Newfoundland, where they are naturally suited to the terrain. Ironically, they are not native to the island. The estimated 150,000 or so that thrive in the province today are descended from a handful of individuals introduced in 1878 and 1904 as a source of meat.

White-Tailed Deer

The color of the white-tailed deer varies with the season but is generally light brown in summer, turning dirty gray in winter. The white-tailed deer's tail is dark on top, but when the animal runs, it holds its tail erect, revealing an all-white underside. White-tails frequent thickets along the rivers and lakes of interior forests.

Black Bears

Black bears number around 8,000-10,000 in Newfoundland and Labrador. Black bears are not always black in color (they can be brown), causing them to be called brown bears when in fact they are not. Their weight varies considerably; males average 150 kilograms and females 100 kilograms. Their diet is omnivorous, consisting primarily of grasses and berries and supplemented by small mammals. They are not true hibernators, but in winter they can sleep for up to a month at a time before changing position. During this time, their heartbeat drops to 10 beats per minute, body temperature drops, and they lose up to 30 percent of their body weight. Females reach reproductive maturity after five years; cubs, usually two, are born in late winter, while the mother is still asleep.

Polar Bears

Polar bears are often sighted along the Labrador coast during the spring breakup of pack ice, but their range is out of reach to most travelers. The one destination renowned for polar bear sightings are the Torngat Mountains in northern Labrador. These largest members of the bear family weigh up to 600 kilograms and measure over three meters from head to toe.

Caribou

Standing 1.5 meters at the shoulder, caribou

have adapted perfectly to the harsh Arctic climate. They weigh up to 150 kilograms and are the only member of the deer family in which both sexes grow antlers. The only region of Atlantic Canada where caribou are present is Newfoundland and Labrador; 12 herds roam the island and are most plentiful in the Avalon Wilderness Reserve and across the Northern Peninsula. Four caribou herds inhabit Labrador, the most famous of which is the George River herd. Its 75,000 caribou migrate eastward from Québec in late spring to calve in Torngat Mountains National Park. This calving ground is currently under consideration for a national park.

Lynx

The elusive lynx is an endangered species across Atlantic Canada. It is present in low numbers in all provinces. Easily identifiable by its pointy black ear tufts and an oversized tabby cat appearance, the animal has broad padded paws that distribute its weight, allowing it to float on a surface of snow. It weighs up to 10 kilograms but appears much larger because of its coat of long, thick fur. The lynx is a solitary creature that prefers the cover of forest, feeding mostly at night on small mammals.

Beavers

One of the animal kingdom's most industrious mammals is the beaver. Growing to a length of 50 centimeters and tipping the scales at around 20 kilograms, it has a flat, rudderlike tail and webbed back feet that enable it to swim at speeds of up to 10 kilometers per hour. Once hunted for their fur, beavers can be found in flat forested areas throughout Atlantic Canada. They build their dam walls and lodges of twigs, branches, sticks of felled trees, and mud. They eat the bark and smaller twigs of deciduous plants and store branches underwater, near the lodge, as a winter food supply.

SEA LIFE

The ocean water that surrounds the four provinces nurtures an astonishing abundance and variety of sea creatures, from tiny uncounted single-celled organisms up through the convoluted links of the food chain to the Earth's largest beings—whales.

Tidal Zones

Along the shores, the same conditions that provide for rich and diverse plants—rocky indented coasts, dramatic tidal variations— also create ideal habitats for varied animal communities in the tidal zone. Between the

black bear

highest and lowest tides, the Maritime shore is divided into six zones, each determined by the amount of time it is exposed to air. The black zone, just above the highest high-water mark, gets its name from the dark band of primitive blue-green algae that grows there. The next zone is called the periwinkle zone, for the small marine snails that proliferate within it. Able to survive prolonged exposure to air, periwinkles can leave the water to graze on the algae. The barnacle zone, encrusted with the tenacious crustaceans, while also exposed several hours daily during low tides, receives the brutal pounding of breaking waves. Next is the rockweed zone—home to mussels, limpets, and hermit crabs (which commandeer the shells of dead periwinkles)—and the comparatively placid Irish moss zone, which shelters and feeds sea urchins, starfish, sea anemones, crabs, and myriad other animals familiar to anyone who has peered into the miniature world of a tide pool. Last is the laminarian zone, where lobsters, sponges, and fishes thrive in the forests of kelp growing in the deep churning water.

Fish

Beyond the tidal zones lie the waters of the continental shelf and then the open sea. Flowing south from the Arctic, cold oxygen-laden currents also carry loads of silica, ground out of the continental granite by the glaciers and poured into the sea by coastal rivers. Oxygen and silica together create an ideal environment for the growth of diatoms, the microscopic one-celled plants that form the bedrock of the ocean's food chain. In the sunlight of long summer days in these northern latitudes, the numbers of diatoms increase exponentially. They are the food source for shrimp and herring, which in turn support larger fish, such as mackerel, Atlantic salmon, and tuna.

Whales

Not all the creatures that swim in the Atlantic Ocean are cold-blooded. About 20 whale species cruise offshore. The so-called baleen or toothless whales—minke, humpback, beluga, and right whales—are lured by the massive food stocks of plankton and tiny shrimp called krill, which the whales strain from the water through their sieve-like curtains of baleen. The toothed whales—a family that includes dolphins, orcas (killer whales), and fin and pilot whales—feed on the vast schools of smelt-like capelin, herring, and squid. In the last three decades, whaling has been halted by Canadian law and international moratoriums, and populations of these beleaguered mammals are undergoing very encouraging comebacks.

Today's lucrative whaling industry is based not on butchering but on simply bringing curious onlookers to observe the wonderful animals up close. The whales that frequent local waters arrive from the Caribbean between June and mid-July and remain through October; the season peaks during August and September. On Newfoundland's western coast, fin, minke, humpback, and pilot whales are sighted on the shores of Gros Morne National Park

Seals

Harp seals, after fattening themselves on fish off the Labrador and Greenland coasts, migrate to northern Newfoundland and the Gulf of St. Lawrence in January and February. The females arrive first, living on the ice and continuing to feed in the gulf before giving birth to their pups. These snowy white, doe-eyed pups became the poster children of the conservation movement in the 1970s. The slaughter of the young pups—carried out by sealers who bashed in their heads with clubs—galvanized protests and finally embarrassed the Canadian government into restricting the killing in the mid-1980s. Even with the Canadian government quietly allowing hunting to resume in 1995, seal numbers have rebounded dramatically in the last two decades, and the current population stands at around five million

BIRDS

If you're an avid birder, Atlantic Canada's bird life may leave you breathless. In addition to hundreds of year-round resident species, the Atlantic migratory route stretches across part of the region, bringing in millions of seasonal visitors for spectacular and sometimes raucous displays.

Large numbers of seabirds, the region's densest concentrations, gather on the coastlines of Newfoundland's Avalon Peninsula, most notably at Cape St. Mary Sea Bird Sanctuary. Species found there include common and arctic terns, kittiwakes, great and double-crested cormorants, Leach's storm-petrels, razorbills, guillemots, murres, gannets, and 95 percent of North America's breeding Atlantic puffins.

Each species has found its niche, and each is remarkable in its own way. The black-and-white murre, for example, is an expert diver that uses its wings as flippers to swim through the water chasing fish. This behavior can sometimes get the birds caught up with the fish in nets. The murre's cousin, the comical-looking Atlantic puffin, borrows the penguin's tuxedo markings but is nicknamed the "sea parrot" for its distinctive triangular red-and-yellow bill. Puffins make Swiss cheese of the land, as they nest in burrows they've either dug out themselves or inherited from predecessors. In Labrador, ruffled and spruce grouse, woodpeckers, ravens, jays, chickadees, nuthatches, and ptarmigans are a few of the inland birds you may spot. Birds of prey include red-tailed, broad-winged, and other hawks; owls and the gyrfalcon.

History

THE EARLIEST INHABITANTS

Atlantic Canada's earliest inhabitants arrived in Labrador about 9,000 years ago, camping near the large rivers and hunting seals and walrus during the summer. Archaeological research documents that these Maritime Archaic people hunted seals and whales along the Strait of Belle Isle and hunted caribou inland around 7500 BC. They eventually crossed the strait to the island of Newfoundland's northern portion and established encampments such as that at Port au Choix, where their burial grounds and artifacts date to 2300 BC. Around 1000 BC, these people died out. A thousand years later, the Dorset people, ancestors of today's Inuit, arrived from the north. They survived until about AD 600. The Beothuk, called Red Indians for their use of ocher in burial rituals, came to Newfoundland around 2,000 years ago.

Mi'kmaq

Culturally and linguistically related to the Algonquian people, the largest language group in Canada, the Mi'kmaq made a home throughout present-day Nova Scotia, New Brunswick, and as far west as Québec. They were coastal dwellers who fished with spears and hook and line while also collecting shellfish from the shoreline. Hunting was of lesser importance for food but earned a great degree of status among other members of the group. Canoes with sails were built for summer travel, while in winter toboggans (a word that originates from the Mi'kmaq word *topaghan*) and snowshoes were essential.

Like aboriginal peoples across North America, the Mi'kmaq practiced a kind of spiritual animism, deeply tied to the land. The trees, animals, and landforms were respected and blessed. Before food could be consumed or a tree felled, for example, it was appreciated for its life-sustaining sacrifice. Mythology also played an important part in spiritual life, along with rituals, shamanism, and potlatch ceremonies.

THE FIRST EUROPEANS

Brendan the Navigator, a fifth-century Irish monk, may have been the first European to explore the area; he sought Hy-Brazil, the "wonderful island of the saints," and later accounts of his voyage, recorded in the medieval bestseller *Navigatio Sancti Brendani,* describe a land with coastal topography similar to Newfoundland's.

Atlantic Canada's link to the Vikings is more certain. Driven out of Scandinavia, it's believed by overpopulation, Norse seafarers settled in Iceland and began to establish settlements in Greenland. Around AD 1000 they sailed in long stout ships, called *knorrs,* southwest from Greenland and down the Labrador coastline, establishing a temporary settlement at L'Anse aux Meadows on Newfoundland's Northern Peninsula. There they built at least eight houses and two boatsheds of cut turf and lived off the land. It is not known how long they lived there, but they stayed long enough to construct a forge for crafting implements from iron ore they dug and smelted. It may have been hostilities with the native people that drove them out. The remnants of their settlement would remain unrecognized until the 1960s.

"Newfoundland" as a place-name originated with the Italian explorer Giovanni Caboto—better known today as John Cabot. Sailing westward from Bristol with a sanction to claim all lands hitherto "unknown to Christians," he sighted the "New Founde Lande" in 1497 and claimed it in the name of his employer, King Henry VII of England. His first landfall probably lay in the northern part of the island. He and his men explored the coast and also sighted Prince Edward Island and Nova Scotia before returning to England. In the summer of 1997, celebrations in St. John's and across Newfoundland commemorated the 500-year anniversary of the event.

The Fabulous Fisheries

So abundant were the cod fisheries of the Grand Banks, the shallow undersea plateaus south and east of Newfoundland, that John Cabot claimed a man had only to lower a basket into the sea to haul it up full. His report exaggerated the truth only slightly. Although the specifics have not been documented, European fishermen are believed to have preceded Cabot by decades. Legends in Newfoundland describe the Basques as whale hunters in the Strait of Belle Isle as early as the 1470s. France's fishing exploits are better known. In the early 1500s, French fleets roamed the seas from the Grand Banks—where they caught cod and dried them on Newfoundland's beaches—to inland rivers such as the salmon-rich Miramichi in what is now New Brunswick. England's fishing fleets were equally active, leading one diplomat to describe Newfoundland as "a great ship moored near the Grand Banks for the convenience of English fishermen."

England also dabbled in other commercial interests in Newfoundland. A group of merchants from England's West Country settled Trinity in the mid-1500s. Cupids, England's first chartered colony on the island, began in 1610. In contrast, St. John's evolved independently and belonged to no nation; the port served as a haven and trading center for all of Europe's fishing fleets and Signal Hill, the lofty promontory beside the harbor, dates as a lookout and signal peak from the early 1500s.

French Interests

Ultimately, France was more interested in trading posts and settlements than in fishing. The French Crown granted Sieur de Monts a monopoly to develop the fur trade, and in 1604 the nobleman-merchant, with explorer Samuel de Champlain, led an exploratory party to the mouth of the Bay of Fundy. The expedition established a camp on an island in the St. Croix River (the river that now separates New Brunswick from Maine). The group barely survived the bitter first winter and relocated across the Bay of Fundy, establishing Port-Royal as a fur-trading post in the Annapolis basin the following spring.

The grant was canceled, and while most of the expedition returned to France in 1607, a group of French settlers took their place at Port-Royal in 1610. The French dubbed the area Acadia, or "Peaceful Land."

The French settlement and others like it ignited the fuse between England and France. John Cabot had claimed the region for England, but explorer Jacques Cartier also claimed many of the same coastlines for France several decades later. For France, the region was choice property, a potential New France in the New World. On the other hand, England's colonial aspirations centered farther south, where colonization had begun at Virginia and Massachusetts. England didn't *need* what is now Atlantic Canada, though the region offered much with its rich fisheries, but it was a place to confront the expansion of the French, England's most contentious enemy in Europe.

In terms of military strength, the British had the upper hand. An ocean separated France from its dream of settlement, while England's military forces and volunteer militias were located along the eastern seaboard. In 1613, a militia from Virginia plundered and burned the buildings at Port-Royal. The French relocated to a more protected site farther up the Annapolis River, built another fort named Port-Royal, and designated it Acadia's colonial capital in 1635.

France's Sphere Develops

The French Acadian settlements quickly spread beyond the Port-Royal area to the Fundy and Minas Basin coastlines. The merchant Nicholas Denys, whose name is entwined with France's early exploration, established fortified settlements on Cape Breton at St. Peters and at Guysborough in 1653. So many Acadians settled at Grand-Pré that it became the largest settlement and the hub of villages in the area. Other settlements were established across Acadia on Cape Breton, the Cobequid Bay and Cape Chignecto coastlines,

and from the Restigouche Uplands to the Baie des Chaleurs, in what is now northern New Brunswick.

France needed a military center, and created it in the mid-1600s at Plaisance, one of the earliest and most important fishing ports on the Avalon Peninsula in Newfoundland. Here, they erected another tribute to the French Crown and named the new fortification Fort Royal.

British reprisals against the French increased. The British hammered Port-Royal again and again, and in 1654, a militia from New England destroyed some of the Acadian settlements. In Newfoundland, France's presence at Plaisance prompted the British to counter by building forts around St. John's in 1675.

The Treaty of Utrecht

Hostilities between England and France in the New World mirrored political events in Europe. Fighting ebbed and flowed across Atlantic Canada as the powers jockeyed for control on the European continent. Queen Anne's War (1701-1713), the War of Austrian Succession (1745-1748), and the Seven Years' War (1756-1763) were all fought in Europe, but corresponding battles between the English and French took place in North America as well (where they were known collectively as the French and Indian Wars).

The Treaty of Utrecht in 1713 settled Queen Anne's War in Europe. Under the terms of the treaty, England fell heir to all of French Acadia (though the borders were vague). In Newfoundland, Plaisance came into British hands and was renamed Castle Hill. The treaty awarded France the token settlements of the offshore Île Saint-Jean (Prince Edward Island) and Île Royale (Cape Breton). Acadia became an English colony. Nova Scotia (New Scotland) rose on the ashes of New France and the fallen Port-Royal; the British took the fort in 1710, renamed it Fort Anne, and renamed the settlement Annapolis Royal. The town was designated the colony's first capital until Halifax was established and became the capital in 1749.

The French military regrouped. It fled from the peninsula and began to build (and never finished) the Fortress of Louisbourg on Île Royale's Atlantic seacoast in 1719. Once again, the French envisioned the fortification as a new Paris and France's major naval base, port city, and trading center in North America. Simultaneously, they sent 300 fishermen and farmers across the Northumberland Strait to create a new settlement at Port-la-Joye; the enclave, at what is now Charlottetown's southwestern outer edge, was intended to serve as the breadbasket for the Fortress of Louisbourg.

The British quickly responded. A fort at Grassy Island on Chedabucto Bay was their first effort, a site close enough to the Fortress of Louisbourg to watch the arrivals and departures of the French fleets. By 1745, Louisbourg represented a formidable threat to England, so the Brits seized the fortress and deported the inhabitants. But no sooner had they changed the flag than the French were moving back in again. The War of Austrian Succession in Europe ended with the Treaty of Aix-la-Chapelle in 1748, which, among other things, returned Louisbourg to France.

Full-Fledged War

Peace was short-lived. Eight years later, in 1756, the Seven Years' War broke out in Europe, and once more both powers geared up for confrontation in Atlantic Canada. Britain's Grassy Island fort was strategically located, but too small a military base. In 1749 a British convoy sailed into capacious Halifax Harbour, established England's military hub in the North Atlantic there, and named Halifax the capital of Nova Scotia. Fort Edward near the Fundy seacoast went up in the midst of an Acadian area and guarded the overland route from Halifax, while Fort Lawrence on the Chignecto Isthmus, between Nova Scotia and New Brunswick, was built to defend the route to the mainland. The fort defiantly faced two of France's most formidable forts: Fort Beauséjour and Fort Gaspéreau.

The stage was set for war, and the region's civilian inhabitants, the Acadian farmers, were trapped in the middle. Decades before, England had demanded but not enforced an oath of allegiance from the Acadians who lived under their jurisdiction. By the 1750s, however, the British decided to demand loyalty, readying a plan to evict the Acadians from their land and replace noncompliant French inhabitants with Anglo settlers. In 1755, the British swept through the region and enforced the oath. In a show of force, more than 2,000 troops from Boston captured Fort Beauséjour and renamed it Fort Cumberland.

The Acadian Deportation

England's actions unleashed chaos. Those who refused to sign the oath of allegiance were rounded up and deported, and their villages and farmlands were burned. By October, 1,100 Acadians had been deported, while others fought the British in guerrilla warfare or fled to the hinterlands of Cape Breton, New Brunswick, and Québec.

The Acadians being deported were herded onto ships bound for the English colonies on the eastern seaboard, or anyplace that would accept them. Some ships docked in England, others in France, and others in France's colonies in the Caribbean. As the ports wearied of the human cargo, many of them refused the vessels entry, and the ships returned to the high seas to search for other ports willing to accept the Acadians. In one of the period's few favorable moments, the Spanish government offered the refugees free land in Louisiana, and many settled there in 1784, where they became known as Cajuns.

Refugee camps, rife with disease and malnutrition, sprang up across the Maritimes. Beaubears Island, on New Brunswick's Miramichi River, began as a refugee center. About 3,500 Acadians fled from Nova Scotia to Île du Saint-Jean (Prince Edward Island); 700 lost their lives on two boats that sank on the journey. Many Acadians returned only to be deported again, some as many as seven or eight times.

Exact deportation numbers are unknown. Historians speculate that 10,000 French inhabitants lived in Acadia in 1755; by the time the deportation had run its course in 1816, only 25 percent of them remained. The poet Henry Wadsworth Longfellow distilled the tragedy in *Evangeline,* a fictional story of two lovers divided by the events.

England's Final Blow

In 1758, the British moved in for the kill. They seized the Fortress of Louisbourg and toppled Port-la-Joye, renaming it Fort Amherst. The French stronghold at Québec fell the next year. In the ultimate act of revenge, the British troops returned to Louisbourg in 1760 and demolished the fortress stone by stone so it would never rise again against England. New France was almost finished; bereft of a foothold in Atlantic Canada, the French launched a convoy from France and captured St. John's in 1762. The British quickly swooped in and regained the port at the Battle of Signal Hill, the final land battle of the Seven Years' War. Finally, the bitter French and Indian Wars were extinguished.

Postwar Developments

Atlantic Canada, as you see it now, then began to take shape. After the British had swept the Acadians from their land, prosperous "planters," gentleman-farmers from New England, were lured to the lush Annapolis Valley with free land grants. Merchants settled Yarmouth in the 1760s, and other Anglo settlers went to Prince Edward Island. The island, formerly part of Nova Scotia, became an English colony in 1769.

Some of the Acadians had evaded capture, and settlements such as the Pubnico communities south of Yarmouth date to the predeportation period. But most of the region's surviving Acadian areas began after the refugees returned and settled marginal lands no one else wanted, such as the rocky seacoast of La Côte Acadienne (the Acadian Coast) in western Nova Scotia.

In Canada, England lucked out. Even its inglorious defeat in the American Revolution benefited the British. Loyalists (Americans loyal to England) by the thousands poured into Nova Scotia and New Brunswick. The influx was so great in Saint John and Fredericton that New Brunswick, originally part of Nova Scotia, became an English colony, and Saint John became the first incorporated city in Canada.

An Uneasy Peace

Even as peace settled across Atlantic Canada, the specter of war loomed again in Europe. Ever wary of their contentious enemy, the British feared a French invasion by Napoleon's navies in Atlantic Canada. In Halifax, the British built up the harbor's defenses at the Halifax Citadel and other sites. At St. John's, the British fortified Signal Hill with the Queen's Battery.

As if Britain didn't have enough problems with the Napoleonic Wars, the War of 1812 was sparked at the same time, as England and the United States wrangled over shipping rights on the high seas. More British fortifications went up, this time across the Bay of Fundy in New Brunswick, with harbor defenses such as the Carleton Martello Tower at Saint John, the blockhouse at St. Andrews, and other strongholds at more than a dozen strategic places.

TOWARD CONFEDERATION

The Napoleonic Wars ended in June 1815 with Napoleon's defeat at Waterloo. Atlantic Canada emerged unscathed. The war years had fostered shipping, and Halifax earned a questionable reputation as the home port of privateers who raided ships on the high seas and returned to port to auction the booty at the harbor. In Newfoundland, many ships had been lost on the treacherous shoals outside

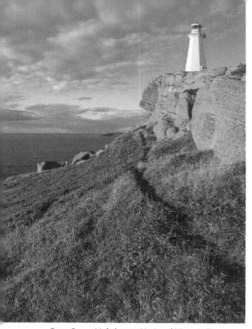

Cape Spear Lighthouse National Historic Site

St. John's Harbour, prompting the British to build the lofty Cape Spear Lighthouse in 1836.

In 1864 a landmark event in Canada's history took place. The "Fathers of the Confederation"—from New Brunswick, Nova Scotia, Prince Edward Island, Ontario, and Québec—met at Province House in Charlottetown. The small city owes its fame as the birthplace of Canada to the discussions of a joint dominion that followed there. In 1867, England gave the union its blessing and signed the British North America Act (now known as the Constitution Act); the Dominion of Canada was born on July 1 as a confederation of Québec, Ontario, New Brunswick, and Nova Scotia united under a parliamentary government.

Under the leadership of its first prime minister, Sir John A. MacDonald, Canada expanded rapidly. The acquisition of Ruperts Land from the Hudson's Bay Company in 1869 increased its total land area sixfold. Manitoba and British Columbia joined the Confederation in 1870 and 1871, respectively.

Prince Edward Island, having initially declined to become a Confederation member, joined the dominion in 1873. Alberta and Saskatchewan followed in 1905, and nearly a half century later, in 1949, Newfoundland became Canada's 10th province.

As a condition of participation in the Confederation, British Columbia and New Brunswick insisted that the government build a railroad across Canada to facilitate trade, transport, and communication. Work on the daunting project began in 1881, and in 1885, just four years later, the last spike was driven in the Canadian Pacific Railway. Linking Vancouver with Montréal, which in turn connected with regional lines in New Brunswick, Nova Scotia, and Prince Edward Island, the railroad united the country in a way no act of confederation could.

World Wars and the Depression

Atlantic Canada became a hotbed of controversy during World War I, when the sensitive issue of Francophone rights was raised. The federal government had decided to initiate a military conscription, and French Canadians were afraid the draft would decrease their already minority population. The measure was a failure, as both French- and English-speaking men of conscription age avoided the draft. By war's end, however, 63,000 Canadians had died in battle, and another 175,000 were wounded. During the war, the nation had supplied Britain with much of its food and also produced large quantities of munitions, ships, and planes—an experience that helped move Canada from a primarily agricultural economy to an industrial one. Afterward, Canada emerged stronger, more independent, and with a greater sense of self-confidence. The Atlantic provinces enjoyed a brief brush with prosperity as mining and manufacturing expanded.

But the Maritimes were not immune to the Great Depression of the 1930s, which hit Canada even harder than the United States. Many businesses collapsed under the financial crisis. When World War II erupted, Canada followed Britain's lead in joining the war against Hitler. Nearly one-tenth of the population of about 11.5 million served in the war effort. Atlantic Canada again took part in shipping many of the munitions and food supplies for the Allies, and the regional and national economies were again revived.

In 1959 the completion of the St. Lawrence Seaway, a project jointly undertaken by the United States and Canada, opened a new sea lane between the Great Lakes and the Atlantic. Three years later, the new TransCanada Highway spanned the country from sea to sea. Linking Vancouver Island with St. John's, Newfoundland, the highway joined all 10 provinces along a single route and made the country just a little smaller.

A Constitution and Autonomy

Starting in 1867, the British North America Act required the British parliament's approval for any Canadian constitutional change. On November 5, 1981, Canada's federal government and the premiers of every province except Québec agreed on a Canadian Constitution and Charter of Rights and Freedoms. The Canada Act formally went into effect on April 17, 1982, removing the last vestiges of the British parliament's control.

Canada remains, however, a member of the Commonwealth.

Old Divisions in Modern Times

The formation of the Parti Québécois in 1968 signaled a popular new militancy among French-speaking separatists in Québec, who desired a political and cultural divorce from the rest of Canada. The Official Languages Act recognized French as the country's second official language after English, but this act only bandaged over deep wounds. Referenda on the question of Québec secession in the 1980s and 1990s have failed to resolve the issue; a provincial vote on the question in 1995 saw the drive for separation defeated by a margin of barely 1 percent. It's difficult to predict which way the pendulum will swing, should there be another vote, but the national government, in any case, has indicated that it will honor the will of the Québécois. In Atlantic Canada, attitudes toward separation are mixed; the general consensus, even in officially bilingual New Brunswick, seems to run in favor of continued Canadian unity, but that consensus is undermined by a growing impatience with Québec's demands for what many Canadians see as preferential treatment from the federal government.

Government and Economy

GOVERNMENT

Canada is a constitutional monarchy. The federation of 10 provinces and three territories operates under a parliamentary democracy in which power is shared between the federal government, based in Ottawa, and the provincial governments. Canada's three nonprovincial territories (Nunavut, Yukon, and the Northwest Territories) exercise delegated—rather than constitutionally guaranteed—authority. The power to make, enforce, and interpret laws rests in the

legislative, executive, and judicial branches of government, respectively.

Federal Government

Under Canada's constitutional monarchy, the formal head of state is the queen of England, who appoints a governor general to represent her for a five-year term. The governor general stays out of party politics and performs largely ceremonial duties, such as opening and closing parliamentary sessions, signing and approving state documents on the queen's behalf, and appointing a temporary replacement if the prime ministry is vacated without warning. The head of government is the prime minister, who is the leader of the majority party or party coalition in the House of Commons.

The country's legislative branch, the Parliament, is comprised of two houses. The House of Commons, with 295 members, is apportioned by provincial population and elected by plurality from the country's districts. The Senate comprises 104 members appointed by the governor general (formerly for a life term, though retirement is now mandatory at age 75) on the advice of the prime minister. Legislation must be passed by both houses and signed by the governor general to become law.

National elections are held whenever a majority party is voted down in the House of Commons or every five years, whichever comes first. Historically, it has been unusual for a government to last its full term.

Provincial and Local Governments

Whereas the federal government has authority over defense, criminal law, trade, banking, and other affairs of national interest, Canada's 10 provincial governments bear responsibility for civil services, health, education, natural resources, and local government. Each of the nation's provincial Legislative Assemblies (in Newfoundland and Labrador, the body is called the House of Assembly) consists of a one-house legislative body with members elected every four years. The nominal head of the provincial government is the lieutenant governor, appointed by the governor general of Canada. Executive power, however, rests with the Cabinet, headed by a premier, the leader of the majority party.

ECONOMY

Traditionally, the economy of Atlantic Canada revolved around resource-based industries such as fishing, forestry, and mining. Although communities established

around fishing and farming areas continue to thrive, the economy today is a lot more diverse. In addition to the stalwarts discussed below, other growing sectors include information technology, the medical field, and the film industry.

Fishing

Canada was once the world's largest fish-exporting country, but poor resource management and overfishing have destroyed its once-bounteous supplies. Newfoundland and Labrador's fisheries, a chronic boom-or-bust industry, contribute some $300 million yearly to the economy, with catches of mackerel, flounder, capelin, herring, squid, eel, fish roe, sole, salmon, perch, turbot, halibut, lobster, and farmed mussels and rainbow trout. Labrador also produces half of Canada's commercial char. Since the 1990s, when the cod industry came to a standstill, Newfoundland fisheries have diversified. Now scallops and shrimp make up a good percentage of the catch.

Natural Resources

Atlantic Canada's fisheries have declined as a consequence of modern fishing methods as well as foreign competition. As a result, the area has turned to its other resources: timber, coal, and other minerals.

Western Labrador's mines contribute about 80 percent of Canada's share of iron ore. Other Newfoundland metals and minerals include copper, lead, zinc, gold, silver, chromium, limestone, gypsum, aluminum silicate, and asbestos. Newfoundland's Avalon Peninsula holds Canada's sole commercial deposit of pyrophyllite, used in the production of ceramics. Newfoundland is economically on the bottom rung of Canada's per-capita income, yet the province is sitting on a gold mine when it comes to natural resources. Offshore oil fields started producing in 2001, and the extraction rate is currently 85 million barrels annually, most of which comes from three offshore fields (Hibernia, Terra Nova, and White Rose).

Power

Water is ubiquitous in the Atlantic provinces (one-third of all the world's freshwater is found in Canada), and hydroelectricity is a cheap, clean export. Québec Hydro alone sells over $1 billion worth of electricity a year to New England.

Tourism

Tourism ranks as the fastest-growing sector of the economy across Atlantic Canada. Most visitors (40 percent) are from the neighboring provinces, while central and western Canada contribute 25 percent, and the United States adds almost 25 percent.

People and Culture

While the topography of this region—the dense forests, mountains, and rugged coastline—has tended to separate people and isolate them in scattered settlements, centuries of sometimes turbulent history have bound the Atlantic Canadians together: the mutual grief of the early wars, the Acadian deportation, immigration upheavals, and the abiding hardships common to resource-based economies. In the same sense, these and other factors have given each population an indisputable identity that makes it difficult to generalize about the diverse peoples of this part of Canada. Senator Eugene Forsey's observations on the country as a whole are equally applicable to Atlantic Canada: "I think our identity will have to be something which is partly British, partly French, partly American, partly derived from a variety of other influences which are too numerous even to catalogue."

In spite of diversity, the region still shares a common identity as a place apart from the rest of Canada. A foreign nation borders it to the southwest, and Atlantic Canada is separated from the body of its nation by the insular bastion of Québec. Although the country began in the east and was nourished by its resources for centuries, Canada's general prosperity has not been fully shared here. Atlantic Canada experiences higher unemployment, higher underemployment, and lower income than any of the other provinces. Unlike the rest of the country, the provinces of Atlantic Canada share economies that rise and fall largely on the vicissitudes of the fisheries and other natural resources.

DEMOGRAPHY

Newfoundland and Labrador, with a population of 527,000, has less than 1.5 people per square kilometer. Ninety-five percent of the population is concentrated on the island of Newfoundland (known as "The Rock").

In Labrador, Inuit, Innu, and Anglo-Labradorians inhabit the sparsely settled eastern coastline and remote central interior. The people of the island of Newfoundland are an overwhelmingly Anglo and Celtic cultural mix (96 percent), whose psyche is linked to the sea and the Grand Banks fisheries. A small number of Mi'kmaq also live on the island.

An insular mentality still informs the provincial character, and more than 60 years after joining the Confederation, residents of The Rock may still refer to their countrymen as "Canadians"—outsiders from another nation. They even inhabit their own time zone, Newfoundland time, a quirky half-hour ahead of Atlantic time.

Though a full-fledged province since 1949, Newfoundland was a colony of England's for centuries. This is why you'll still hear a clipped King's English accent in St. John's, a West Country dialect in some of the small remote fishing villages (called outports), and a softly brushed Irish brogue on the Avalon Peninsula. Some 60 dialects and subdialects have been documented throughout the province, many of them incorporating colorful expressions and vocabulary that are unique to Newfoundland. In addition, the map of the province is decorated with one-of-a-kind place-names: Blow Me Down, Joe Batt's Arm, Happy Adventure, Jerry's Nose, and dozens of other toponymic oddities.

NATIVE PEOPLES AND MÉTIS

The first European explorers to reach North America found a land that was anything but uninhabited Tribes or nations of aboriginals had been here for millennia, from coast to coast and up into the continent's subarctic and Arctic regions.

Various names are used to describe aboriginal Canadians, and all can be correct in context. The government still uses the term *Indian,* despite its links to Christopher Columbus and the misconception that he had landed in India. *Native* is generally considered acceptable only when used in conjunction with *people, communities,* or *leaders.* *Indigenous* and *aboriginal* can have insulting connotations when used in certain contexts.

Mi'kmaq

When Europeans first arrived, perhaps 20,000 Mi'kmaq lived in the coastal areas of the Gaspé Peninsula and the Maritimes east of the Saint John River. The name Mi'kmaq (also Micmac) is thought to have derived from the word *nikmaq,* meaning "my kin-friends," which early French settlers used as a greeting for the tribe. Mi'kmaq historically referred to themselves as Lnu (meaning "human being" or "the people"). The aboriginal Mi'kmaq fished and hunted, and became involved with the fur trade in the 18th century.

The Mi'kmaq historically had practiced little or no agriculture, and attempts by the British to convert them into farmers fared poorly. Later, they found employment building railways and roads and in lumbering and fisheries. Today the Mi'kmaq number an estimated 15,000 in the Maritime provinces, Newfoundland, and parts of New England.

Inuit

The Inuit (formerly known as Eskimos—a name many consider pejorative) inhabit the northern regions of Canada, as well as Alaska and Greenland. Their ancestors arrived in the Arctic in the 11th century. Today they number roughly 25,000 in eight main tribal groups and share a common language—Inuktitut—with six dialects. Until the late 1930s, when a court ruled that their welfare was the responsibility of the federal government, the Inuit were largely ignored by Canada, principally because they occupied inhospitable lands in the far north.

In the late 18th century, Moravian missionaries in Labrador established the first lasting contact with the Inuit, followed by commercial whalers and explorers. The Europeans initiated cultural and technological changes in the traditional societies (including almost universal conversion to Christianity) that continue to this day. Although the Inuit of northern Labrador gained self-governing status with the creation of Nunatsiavut in 2005, they continue to live in small remote settlements while maintaining traditional practices: hunting seals, caribou, and whales, and continuing other aspects of Inuit culture.

Métis

The progeny of native people and Caucasians, the Métis (named for an old French word meaning "mixed") form a diverse and complex group throughout Canada. They date from the time of earliest European contact: in Atlantic Canada, unions between European fishermen and native women—sometimes casual, sometimes formal—produced Métis offspring by the early 1600s.

In the 17th century, the French government encouraged this mixing, seeing it as conducive to converting the native people to Christianity and more speedily increasing the population of New France. Samuel de Champlain said, "Our young men will marry your daughters, and we shall be one people." That policy had changed by the 1700s, however, and France then *discouraged* mixed unions, in part because of the increased presence of European women in North America. This policy led to the development of distinct Métis settlements, mainly around the Great Lakes (these settlements would later grow into cities such as Chicago, Milwaukee, Sault Ste. Marie, and Detroit).

Some identify themselves with the aboriginals, some with Whites, while others consider themselves members of a society and culture distinct from both.

LANGUAGE

Although Canada is constitutionally bilingual, English is the language of choice for most of the country and for the majority of Atlantic Canadians. (In 2016, French was the mother tongue of about 22 percent of Canadians, while the figure in Québec was 88 percent.) The Official Languages Acts of 1969 and 1988 established French and English as equal official languages and designated rights for minority language speakers throughout the country.

In Atlantic Canada, English is the first language for the majority. Francophones are smaller minorities in Newfoundland (less than 1 percent). The Inuit of Labrador continue to speak Inuktitut.

Canada, Eh!

Canadian English is subtly different from American English, not only in pronunciation but also in lexicon. For instance, Canadians may say "serviette," "depot," and "chesterfield" where Americans would say "napkin," "station," and "couch." Spelling is a bit skewed as well, as Canadians have kept many British spellings—colour, kilometre, centre, and cheque, for example. "Eh?" is a common lilt derived from British and Gaelic in which each sentence ends on a high note, as though a question had been asked. At the same time, Canadian English has been profoundly influenced by its neighbor to the south. Nevertheless, language variations pose no serious threat to communication.

RELIGION

Atlantic Canada's cultural diversity is also reflected in religion. Though Christian faiths have predominated since the first Europeans settled here, and despite Canada's less-than-sterling history of religious tolerance, the Maritime territories have offered sects and a variety of denominations—including oppressed minority groups such as Mennonites, Doukhobors, Eastern European and Russian Jews, and others—an opportunity to start anew. The domination of organized religions (primarily the Roman Catholic Church and various Protestant churches) over the lives of Canadians has waned substantially since the 1960s. Partly this is due to the overall national drop in church membership over the past several decades, but it could also be an effect of Canada's increasingly multicultural population. In the Atlantic provinces, church affiliation is still high, and the Catholic and Protestant churches, in particular, still play substantial roles in the lives and communities of people throughout the region.

Essentials

Transportation............... 122

Recreation..................... 124

Accommodations............. 127

Travel Tips 130

Health and Safety...... 131

Information and Services 133

Transportation

GETTING THERE

Visitors to Atlantic Canada have the option of arriving by road, rail, ferry, or air. The main gateway city for flights from North America and Europe is Halifax (Nova Scotia), from where flights leave for other provincial capitals.

Air

Most long-haul international and domestic flights into eastern Canada set down at Toronto, Ottawa, or Montréal, with connecting or ongoing flights to Atlantic Canada.

AIR CANADA

Air Canada (888/247-2262, www.aircanada.com) is one of the world's largest airlines, serving five continents. The company has one of the world's easiest-to-understand fare systems, with five fare levels and multiple ways of searching for online flights and fares. It offers direct flights to Halifax from Fredericton, Saint John, Moncton, St. John's, Montréal, Ottawa, Toronto, Calgary, and Boston. All other flights from North America are routed through Toronto, Ottawa, or Montréal, where connections can be made to Halifax. From Europe, Air Canada flies from London to Halifax. From the South Pacific, Air Canada operates flights from Sydney to Vancouver for onward connections to Halifax. Asian cities served by direct Air Canada flights include Beijing, Hong Kong, Nagoya, Osaka, Seoul, Shanghai, Taipei, and Tokyo. All terminate in Vancouver. Air Canada's flights originating in South America are all routed through Toronto.

WESTJET

Canada's second-largest airline, **WestJet** (403/250-5839 or 888/937-8538, www.westjet.com), is the main competition to Air Canada. Based in Calgary, its flights extend as far east as St. John's, with flights routed through Toronto to Halifax, Fredericton, Moncton, Charlottetown, Deer Lake, and St. John's.

U.S. AIRLINES

Air Canada offers direct daily flights from Boston to Halifax, but the city is also served by **Delta** (800/221-1212, www.delta.com) from New York (LGA); **American** (800/433-7300, www.aa.com) from Philadelphia; and **United** (800/538-2929, www.united.com) from Chicago and Newark. Delta also flies between New York and Charlottetown and United between New York and St. John's.

Car

Labrador can be reached from Québec on Highway 389, from Baie-Comeau, on the St. Lawrence River's northern bank. The 581-kilometer drive takes nine hours; the two-lane road wends through Québec's northern wilderness to enter western Labrador at Labrador City.

GETTING AROUND

Driving, whether it be your own vehicle or a rental car, is by far the best way to get around Atlantic Canada. This section talks about driving in Canada, as well as public transportation options.

Air

St. John's. **Air Canada** (888/247-2262, www.aircanada.ca) and its subsidiary, Rouge, saturate the region with frequent flights. **WestJet**

Air Taxes

The Canadian government collects a variety of "departure taxes" on all flights originating from Canada. These taxes are generally not in the advertised fare, but they will all be included in the ticket purchase price. First up is the **Air Travellers Security Charge**, $7-14 each way for flights within North America and $25 round-trip for international flights. At the time of writing, both major Canadian airlines were adding $25-100 per domestic sector for a fuel surcharge and $3 for an insurance surcharge. Although fees were reduced in 2016, **NAV Canada** still dips its hand in your pocket, collecting $9-20 per flight to maintain the country's navigational systems. Additionally, passengers departing Halifax International Airport must pay an **Airport Improvement Fee** of $25, while those departing Bathurst (New Brunswick) pay $40, the highest such fee in Canada. Additionally, if your flight transits through Toronto, you pay a $4 improvement fee for that airport.

routes between North Sydney (Nova Scotia) and Newfoundland. The shorter passage, to Port-aux-Basques, takes 5-6 hours (adult $44, senior $40, child $20, vehicle under 20 feet $115). Summer-only sailings between North Sydney and Argentia take around 14 hours (adult $125, senior $115, child $62, and from $253 for vehicles).

The **Department of Transportation and Works** (www.tw.gov.nl.ca) operates ferries on 16 routes within Newfoundland to Labrador. The region's most adventurous ferry trip is the 4.5-day round-trip to remote Nain operated by **Nunatsiavut Marine** (709/896-2262 or 855/896-2262, www.labradorferry.ca).

Driving in Canada

U.S. and International Driver's Licenses are valid in Canada. All highway signs give distances in kilometers and speeds in kilometers per hour (km/h). Unless otherwise posted, the maximum speed limit on the highways is 100 kilometers per hour (62 miles per hour).

Infants weighing up to nine kilograms must be strapped into a "bucket"-style car seat. Use of a child car seat for larger children weighing 9-18 kilograms is also required. Before venturing north of the 49th parallel, U.S. residents should ask their vehicle insurance company for a Canadian Non-resident Inter-provincial Motor Vehicle Liability Insurance Card. You may also be asked to prove vehicle ownership, so be sure you have your vehicle registration form.

If you're a member in good standing of an automobile association, take your membership card—the Canadian AA provides members of related associations full services, including free maps, itineraries, excellent tour books, road- and weather-condition information, accommodations reservations, travel agency services, and emergency road services. For more information, contact the **Canadian Automobile Association** (613/247-0117, www.caa.ca)

(403/250-5839 or 888/937-8538, www.westjet.com) also flies between all major Atlantic Canada cities.

PAL Airlines (709/576-1666 or 800/563-2800, www.palairlines.ca) serves all of Newfoundland and Labrador with direct flights into the province from Halifax and Montreal. **Air Labrador** (709/758-0002 or 800/563-3042, www.airlabrador.com) links the remote towns of Labrador to the outside world, flying in from St. John's, Deer Lake, and Montréal.

Air travel is the public transportation mode of choice throughout the provinces. While the airlines haven't put bus or ferry travel (or trains, yet) out of business, the airports are usually crowded and regional flights are often filled.

Ferry

Marine Atlantic (902/794-5254 or 800/341-7981, www.marine-atlantic.ca) operates two

Note: Drinking and driving (with a blood-alcohol level of 0.08 percent or higher) in Atlantic Canada can get you imprisoned for up to five years on a first offense and will cost you your license for at least 12 months. Those caught driving with a blood alcohol level between 0.05 and 0.08 percent automatically lose their license for seven days.

CAR RENTAL

Major rental companies include the following: **Avis** (800/331-1212, www.avis.ca), **Budget** (800/268-8900, www.budget.ca), **Enterprise** (800/261-7331, www.enterprise. com), **National** (877/222-9058, www.nationalcar.com), and **Thrifty** (800/847-4389, www. thrifty.com).

Recreation

In Atlantic Canada's great outdoors, just about every form of recreation is feasible and first-rate: bicycling and hiking, mountaineering, scuba diving, houseboating, river rafting and canoeing, ocean and river kayaking, sailing, windsurfing, rockhounding, bird-watching, fishing, hockey, tennis, golf—you name it. No matter what the temperature—35°C (95°F) in summer or -15°C (5°F) in winter—people can be found enjoying some form of recreation throughout the year.

Spectator sports popular in the Atlantic provinces include minor-league professional ice hockey, harness racing, and rugby.

PARKS

The region's national and provincial parks come in a wide range of personalities and offer an equally eclectic array of activities and facilities.

National Parks

Newfoundland and Labrador has three parks—**Terra Nova,** renowned among kayakers; **Gros Morne,** where spectacular cliffs rise above inland "ponds"; and **Torngat Mountains,** protecting the remote northern tip of Labrador.

For information on these parks, including detailed trip planners, visit the **Parks Canada** website (www.pc.gc.ca).

Provincial Parks

Protecting areas of natural, historical, and cultural importance, Atlantic Canada's many

hundreds of provincial parks also provide a wide variety of recreational opportunities. All provide day-use facilities such as picnic areas and washrooms, while many also have playgrounds, canoe rentals, and concessions. A good number also have campgrounds and summer interpretive programs.

You'll find lots of information about provincial parks at local information centers and in general tourism literature. You can also contact the Department of Environment and Conservation, 709/729-2664, www.env.gov. nl.ca/parks.

HIKING

Hiking is one of the most popular activities in Atlantic Canada. Not only are there hundreds of trails to explore, but it's free and anyone can do it. Hiking in Newfoundland and Labrador is relegated, for the most part, to the height of summer, except for the hardiest adventurers. Coastal areas throughout Atlantic Canada are generally free of pesky insects, but insect repellent is wise inland from May through September. As national and provincial parks protect the most spectacular scenery, it'll be no surprise that this is where you find the best hiking.

FISHING

Sportfishing in Atlantic Canada is legendary, especially for Atlantic salmon in Newfoundland and Labrador. Fishing guides, tours, lodges (from rustic to luxurious), and packages are available throughout these

National Park Passes

Permits are required for entry in to all Canadian national parks. These are sold at park gates, at all park information centers, and at campground fee stations.

Day passes (less than $10 per person) are the best deal for short visits, but if you're planning to visit a number of parks throughout Atlantic Canada, consider an annual **Parks Canada Discovery Pass,** good for entry into all of Canada's national parks and national historic sites for one year from the date of purchase. The cost is adu t $67.70, senior $57.90, child $33.30, up to a maximum of $136.40 per vehicle. For more information on park passes, check the Parks Canada website (www.pc.gc.ca).

regions. Expect to pay $250-500 a day for a guide. An all-inclusive week's package has the highest price and usually includes license fees, lodging, meals, a guide, and, for remote locations, fly-in transportation. Typical is Labrador's **Rifflin' Hitch Lodge,** a 50-minute flight southeast from Goose Bay (www.rifflinhitchlodge.com). Located on the Eagle River, one of the richest Atlantic salmon rivers in North America, the lodge supplies anglers with some of the world's best fishing and all the comforts of home. Guests enjoy luxuries such as gourmet meals and a hot tub, comfortable private rooms, and fishing from the shore or boats at a ratio of one guide to every two guests.

Salmon

Just one species of salmon is native to the tidal waters of Atlantic Canada—the Atlantic salmon. It is anadromous, spending its time in both freshwater and saltwater. The salmon spend up to three years in local rivers before undergoing massive internal changes that allow them to survive in saltwater. They then spend 2-3 years in the open water, traveling as far as Greenland. After reaching maturity,

they begin the epic journey back to their birthplace, to the exact patch of gravel on the same river from where they emerged. It is the returning salmon that are most sought after by anglers. Atlantic salmon grow to 36 kilograms, although their landlocked relatives rarely exceed 10 kilograms.

Other Saltwater Species

Flounder are caught in shallow waters, where they bury themselves in the sand. Growing to 40 centimeters long, these groundfish are easily caught, and just as easy to lose. Clams and worms are favored baits. **Mackerel,** living in shallow waters throughout summer, are easy to catch using spinning rods.

Freshwater Fish

Speckled trout (also known as brook trout) are widespread throughout the region and are fun to catch and tasty to eat. They tend to gravitate to cooler water, such as spring-fed streams, and can be caught on spinners or flies. Introduced in the late 1800s, **rainbow trout** are in lakes and rivers across Atlantic Canada. Many easily accessible lakes across Atlantic Canada are stocked with trout each spring. Most are rainbows because they are easy to raise and adapt to varying conditions. You can catch them on artificial flies, small spinners, or spoons. The biggest of the species are in Newfoundland and Labrador. Introduced from Europe, **brown trout** are found in some streams and larger lakes, with the regional record a 13-kilogram fish caught in Newfoundland.

Long and lean, **striped bass** inhabit rivers and estuaries throughout the region. There is a definite art to catching the species—it is estimated it takes an average of 40-50 hours of fishing to catch one. Common throughout North America, **whitefish** are easily caught in most rivers and lakes although they rarely exceed 15 centimeters in length.

Fishing Licenses and Regulations

Contact the **Department of Environment**

A Photographer's Dream

Atlantic Canada has incredible light for photography. The sky turns from a Wedgwood color to sapphire blue—a beautiful background for seacoast photographs. Rise at dawn to take advantage of the first rays of sunlight hitting picturesque villages such as **Battle Harbour** in Labrador. Nature photographers will revel in the fall colors of Newfoundland's rugged **Gros Morne National Park.**

While photography is simplest when the weather is favorable—and that's more often than not—don't pass up a morning basking in thick mist, as bright sun illuminates the sky behind the thick clouds. The fog breaks apart gradually, and when it does, the sun radiates like a spotlight, illuminating the sparkling dampness that briefly clings to the landscape.

and Conservation (www.env.gov.nl.ca) for information on fishing in both fresh and tidal waters. A license for trout angling is $8 per year, while a nonresident salmon license costs $53. An important point to note is that non-residents are prohibited from fishing farther than 800 meters from a provincial highway without a guide or direct relative resident.

Fishing in **national parks** requires a separate license, which is available from park offices and some sports shops near major parks ($9.80 for a seven-day license, $34.30 for an annual license).

CYCLING AND MOUNTAIN BIKING

Reasonably good roads and gorgeous scenery make Atlantic Canada excellent road biking territory, while mountain biking has caught on among the adventurous as a way to explore more remote areas of the region. Except on main arteries, particularly the TransCanada Highway, car traffic is generally light. Cyclists, nonetheless, should remain vigilant: Narrow lanes and shoulders are common, and in some areas, drivers may be unaccustomed to sharing the road with bicycles.

Many shops rent decent- to good-quality road and mountain bikes, but if you plan to do some serious riding, you'll probably want to bring your own. An outstanding information resource is **Atlantic Canada Cycling** (902/423-2453, www.atlanticcanadacycling. com). The organization publishes extensive information on cycling routes (including descriptions and ratings of highways and byways throughout Atlantic Canada), tours, races, clubs, and equipment, while its website has links to local operators and a message board.

Guided Tours

Nova Scotia-based **Freewheeling Adventures** (902/857-3600 or 800/672-0775, www.freewheeling.ca) leads agreeable guided trips in small groups, each accompanied by a support van to carry the luggage and, if necessary, the weary biker. Owners Cathy and Philip Guest plan everything—snacks, picnics, and meals at restaurants en route, as well as overnights at country inns. Expect to pay around $300-400 per person per day for the all-inclusive tour. The trips pass through some of Atlantic Canada's prettiest countryside, including Newfoundland's Northern Peninsula.

WATER SPORTS

This ocean-bound region has no shortage of beaches, and most waterside provincial parks have a supervised **swimming** area. With so much water surrounding and flowing through the provinces, **boating** opportunities are nearly infinite.

Canoeing is a traditional form of transportation that remains extremely popular throughout Atlantic Canada. You can rent canoes at many of the more popular lakes. If you bring your own, you can slip into any body of water whenever you please, taking in the scenery and viewing wildlife from water level. Coastal kayaking is another adventure.

WINTERTIME SPORTS

Winter is definitely low season for tourism in Atlantic Canada. Outdoor recreation is severely limited by the weather, although snow-related sports are popular with the locals. In addition to downhill skiing and boarding, skating on frozen ponds is popular, while locals cheer for minor-league ice hockey teams scattered throughout the region.

The region's national parks and many of the provincial parks stay open year-round. In winter, hiking routes are transformed by snow into excellent cross-country ski trails, many of which are groomed by local ski clubs that charge a nominal fee for their use.

SPECTATOR SPORTS

Although the region is home to no National Hockey League (NHL) teams, the exploits of the Toronto Maple Leafs, Montréal Canadiens, and other NHL franchises are passionately followed here. You can also see lively play from NHL-affiliate team the St. John's IceCaps. The season runs October-March; check with local tourist information offices for game schedules and ticket information.

SHOPPING
Business Hours

Shopping hours are generally Monday-Saturday 9am-6pm, with city malls open on Sundays also. Late shopping in most tourist areas is available until 9pm on Thursday and Friday, and supermarkets open 24 hours are found in the larger cities. Generally, banks are open Monday-Wednesday 10am-4pm and Thursday-Friday 10am-5pm. A few banks may open on Saturday, but all are closed on Sunday.

Accommodations

Atlantic Canada has all the chain hotels you know, as well as a range of accommodations that showcase the region—historic B&Bs, grand resorts, riverside cottages, and luxurious fishing lodges. This section will give you a taste of the choices and some hints on reserving a room.

Lodging Reservations

Many large local, national, and international hotel, resort, and motel groups have properties in Atlantic Canada; if you want to make advance reservations at any of their lodgings, simply phone the toll-free reservation center or book online using their websites.

HOTELS, MOTELS, AND RESORTS

International, Canadian, and regional lodging chains are represented in Atlantic Canada. At the more expensive properties, expect all the requisite amenities and services—swimming pools, air-conditioning, in-room Internet access, room service, complimentary toiletries, restaurants, and bars. This type of accommodation can be found in central locations in all cities and major tourist areas. Rates at four- or five-star hotels start at $150 s or d in high season. Prices for a basic motel room in a small town start at $65 s or d, rising to $140 for a room in a chain hotel within walking distance of a major city's downtown core.

The big chains are represented in Atlantic Canada, as well as the following, which you may not be familiar with.

Choice Hotels Canada

Over 300 properties across Canada are marketed under the Choice Hotels (800/424-6423, www.choicehotels.ca) banner. It operates 10 brands, including Sleep, with smallish but clean, comfortable, and inexpensive rooms;

Accommodation Deals

Rates quoted through this guidebook are for a standard double room in the high season (usually July and August, but sometimes as early as June and as late as September). Almost all accommodations are less expensive outside of these busy months, with some discounting their rates by up to 50 percent. You'll enjoy the biggest seasonal discounts at properties that rely on summer tourists.

While you have no influence on the seasonal and weekday/weekend pricing differences detailed above, *how* you reserve a room *can* make a difference in how much you pay. First and foremost, when it comes to searching out actual rates, the Internet is an invaluable tool. All hotel websites listed in this book show rates, and many have online reservation forms. Use these websites to search out specials, many of which are available only on the Internet. Don't be afraid to negotiate during slower times. Even if the desk clerk has no control over rates, there's no harm in asking for a bigger room or one with a better view. Just look for a vacancy sign hanging out front.

Most hotels offer auto association members an automatic 10 percent discount, and whereas senior discounts apply only to those older than 60 or 65 on public transportation and at attractions, most hotels offer discounts to those age 50 and older, with chains such as Best Western also allowing senior travelers a late checkout. "Corporate Rates" are a lot more flexible than in years past; some hotels require nothing more than the flash of a business card for a 10-20 percent discount.

When it comes to frequent-flyer programs, you really do need to be a frequent flyer to achieve free flights, but the various loyalty programs offered by hotels often provide benefits simply for signing up.

Comfort, where guests enjoy a light breakfast and newspaper with a no-frills room; Quality, a notch up in quality with a restaurant and lounge; and Econo Lodge, older properties that have been renovated to Choice's standard and often have a pool and restaurant.

Delta Hotels and Resorts

Owned by Marriott company but still branded by their Canadian name, at Delta Hotels and Resorts expect expect fine hotels with splendid facilities in notable downtown settings. Located in St. John's, Newfoundland. Reservations can be made by calling 888/236-2427 or online at www.marriott.com. Check the Marriott website for package deals offered year-round.

BED-AND-BREAKFASTS

Styles run the gamut from historic mansions to rustic farmhouses, and as a result, amenities can also vary greatly. Regardless, guests can expect hearty home cooking, a peaceful atmosphere, personal service, knowledgeable hosts, and conversation with like-minded travelers. B&Bs are usually private residences, with hosts that live on-site and up to eight guest rooms. As the name suggests, breakfast is included in quoted rates; ask before booking whether it is a cooked or continental breakfast. Rates fluctuate enormously—from $55 s, $65 d for a spare room in an otherwise regular family home to over $200 in a historic mansion.

Reservations

My favorite B&Bs are recommended within the travel chapters of this book. You can also use provincial accommodations guides and local information centers to find out about individual properties. **Select Atlantic Inns** (www.selectinns.ca) is an organization of mid- to top-end B&Bs, with online reservations and lots of information on specific properties. The **Canadian Bed and Breakfast Guide** (www.canadianbandbguide.ca) is a regularly updated database, although listings aren't recommendations as such. Finally, **Bed and Breakfast Online** (www.bbcanada.com) doesn't take bookings, but links are provided, and an ingenious search engine helps you find the accommodation that best fits your needs.

Before reserving a room, it is important to ask a number of questions of your hosts. The two obvious ones are whether or not you'll have your own bathroom and how payment can be made (many establishments don't accept debit cards or all credit cards).

BACKPACKER ACCOMMODATIONS

As accommodation prices are reasonable throughout Atlantic Canada, there is less of a need to find a dorm bed than in other parts of North America. While privately operated backpacker lodges come and go with predictable regularity, Hostelling International operates in this region.

Hostelling International

The curfews and chores are long gone in this worldwide nonprofit organization of 4,200 hostels in 60 countries. Hostelling International Canada has hostels in Newfoundland and Labrador at St. John's, Trinity, Bonavista, and Botwood.

For a dorm bed, members of Hostelling International pay $22-30 per night, nonmembers pay $26-34. Generally, you need to provide your own sleeping bag or linen, but most hostels supply extra bedding (if needed) at no charge. Accommodations are in dormitories (2-10 beds), although single and double rooms are often available for an additional charge. Each hostel also offers a communal kitchen, a lounge area, and laundry facilities, while some have wireless Internet access, bike rentals, and organized tours.

You don't *have* to be a member to stay in an affiliated hostel of Hostelling International, but membership pays for itself after only a few nights of discounted lodging. Aside from discounted rates, benefits of membership vary from country to country but often include discounted air, rail, and bus travel; discounts on car rental; and discounts on some attractions and commercial activities. For Canadians, the

membership charge is $35 annually, or $175 for a Friend Membership (lifetime). For more information, contact HI-Canada (604/684-7111, www.hihostels.ca).

Joining the Hostelling International affiliate of your home country entitles you to reciprocal rights in Canada, as well as around the world; click through the links at www.hihostels.com to your country of choice.

CAMPING

Camping out is a popular summer activity across Atlantic Canada, and you'll find campgrounds in all national parks, many provincial parks, on the outskirts of cities and towns, and in most resort areas. Facilities at park campgrounds vary considerably, but most commercial operations have showers and water, electricity, and sewer hookups.

National parks provide some of the nicest surroundings for camping. All sites have picnic tables, fire grates, toilets, and fresh drinking water, although only some provide showers. Prices range $18-38, depending on facilities and services. A percentage of sites can be reserved through the **Parks Canada Campground Reservation Service** (877/737-3783, www.pccamping.ca). Backcountry camping in a national park costs $8 per person per night.

Private campgrounds are generally located in popular tourist areas and open between May and October. Prices range dramatically, with tent sites from $20, but expect to pay up to $60 for an oceanfront site with all services.

Whenever possible, reservations for campsites—especially at the national parks and most popular provincial parks—should be made at least six weeks in advance. Most provincial parks, however, do not accept reservations, but instead assign sites on a first-come, first-served basis. At those parks, it's best to arrive before noon to ensure yourself a spot. Most provincial parks are open mid-May to mid-October. Most privately owned campsites accept reservations, which are more likely to be held if you send a small deposit.

Travel Tips

EMPLOYMENT AND STUDY

International visitors wishing to work or study in Canada must obtain authorization *before* entering the country. Authorization to work will only be granted if no qualified Canadians are available for the work in question. Applications for work and study are available from all Canadian embassies and must be submitted with a nonrefundable processing fee. The Canadian government has a reciprocal agreement with Australia for a limited number of **holiday work visas** to be issued each year. Australian citizens aged 30 and younger are eligible; contact your nearest Canadian embassy or consulate. For general information on immigrating to Canada, check the **Citizenship and Immigration Canada** website (www.cic.gc.ca).

VISITORS WITH DISABILITIES

A lack of mobility should not deter you from traveling to Atlantic Canada, but you should definitely do some research before leaving home.

If you haven't traveled extensively, start by doing some research at the website of the **Access-Able Travel Source** (www.accessable.com) where you will find databases of specialist travel agencies and lodgings in Canada that cater to travelers with disabilities. **Flying Wheels Travel** (612/381-1622 or 877/451-5006, www.flyingwheelstravel.com) caters solely to the needs of travelers with disabilities. The **Society for Accessible Travel and Hospitality** (212/447-7284, www.sath.org) supplies information on tour operators, vehicle rentals, specific destinations, and companion services. For frequent travelers, the membership fee (US$49 per year) is well worth it. *Emerging Horizons* (www.emerginghorizons.com) is a U.S. quarterly online magazine dedicated to travelers with special needs.

Access to Travel (www.accesstotravel.gc.ca) is an initiative of the Canadian government that includes information on travel within and between Canadian cities. For vision-impaired visitors, **CNIB** (www.cnib.ca) offers a wide range of services from its Halifax office (902/453-1480 or 800/563-2642). Finally, **Spinal Cord Injury Canada** (www.spinalcordinjurycanada.ca) is another good source of information; a provincial head office is located in St. John's (www.sci-nl.ca).

TRAVELING WITH CHILDREN

Regardless of whether you're traveling with toddlers or teens, you will come upon decisions affecting everything from where you stay to your choice of activities. Luckily for you, Atlantic Canada is very family-friendly, with indoor and outdoor attractions aimed specifically at the younger generation.

Admission prices for children are included throughout the travel chapters of this book. As a general rule, reduced prices are for those ages 6 to 16. For two adults and two-plus children, always ask about family tickets. Children under 6 nearly always get in free. Most hotels and motels will happily accommodate children, but always try to reserve your room in advance and let the reservations desk know the ages of your brood. Often, children stay free in major hotels, and in the case of some major chains—such as Holiday Inn—eat free also. Generally, B&Bs aren't suitable for children, and in some cases they don't accept kids at all. Ask ahead.

Let the children help you plan your trip; look at websites and read up on Atlantic Canada together. To make your vacation more enjoyable if you'll be spending a lot of time on the road, rent a minivan (all major rental agencies have a supply). Don't forget to bring along favorite toys and games from home—whatever you think will keep your kids entertained when the joys of sightseeing wear off.

The various provincial tourism websites have sections devoted to children's activities within each province. Another handy source of online information is **Traveling Internationally with Your Kids** (www.travelwithyourkids.com).

WHAT TO PACK

You'll find little use for a suit and tie in Atlantic Canada. Instead, pack for the outdoors. At the top of your must-bring list should be **hiking boots.** Even in summer, you should be geared up for a variety of weather conditions, especially at the change of seasons or if you'll be spending time along the coast. Do this by preparing to **dress in layers,** including at least one pair of fleece pants and a heavy long-sleeved top. For breezy coastal sightseeing, a sweater or windbreaker, hat, sunscreen, and comfortable shoes with rubber soles will come in handy. For dining out, **casual dress** is accepted at all but the most upscale restaurants.

Electrical appliances from the United States work in Canada but those from other parts of the world will require a **current converter** (transformer) to bring the voltage down. Many travel-size shavers, hair dryers, and irons have built-in converters.

Health and Safety

Atlantic Canada is a healthy place. To visit, you don't need to get any vaccinations or booster shots. And when you arrive, you can drink the water from the faucet and eat the food without worry.

If you need an ambulance, call 911 or the number listed on the inside front cover of local telephone directories. All cities and most larger towns have hospitals—look in each travel chapter of this book for locations and telephone numbers.

INSURANCE AND PRESCRIPTIONS

Intraprovincial agreements cover the medical costs of Canadians traveling across the nation. As a rule, the usual health insurance plans from other countries do not include medical care costs incurred while traveling; ask your insurance company or agent if supplemental health coverage is available, and if it is not, arrange for coverage with an independent carrier before departure. Hospital charges vary from place to place but can be as much as $3,000 a day, and some facilities impose a surcharge for nonresidents. Some Canadian companies offer coverage specifically aimed at visitors.

If you're on medication, take adequate supplies with you, and get a prescription from your doctor to cover the time you will be away. You may not be able to get a prescription filled at Canadian pharmacies without visiting a Canadian doctor, so don't wait till you've almost run out. If you wear glasses or contact lenses, ask your optometrist for a spare prescription in case you break or lose your lenses, and stock up on your usual cleaning supplies.

GIARDIA

Giardiasis, also known as "beaver fever," is a real concern for those who drink water from backcountry water sources. It's caused by an intestinal parasite, *Giardia lamblia,* that lives in lakes, rivers, and streams. Once ingested, its effects, although not instantaneous, can be dramatic: severe diarrhea, cramps, and nausea are the most common. Preventive measures should always be taken and include boiling all water for at least 10 minutes, treating all water with iodine, or filtering all water using a filter with a small enough pore size to block the *Giardia* cysts.

WINTER TRAVEL

Travel through Atlantic Canada during winter months should not be undertaken lightly. Before setting out in a vehicle, check antifreeze levels, and always carry a spare tire and blankets or sleeping bags.

Frostbite can occur in a matter of seconds if the temperature falls below freezing and if the wind is blowing. Layer your clothing for the best insulation against the cold, and don't forget gloves and, most important, a warm hat, which can offer the best protection against heat loss. Frostbite occurs in varying degrees. Most often it leaves a numbing, bruised sensation, and the skin turns white. Exposed areas of skin, such as the nose and ears, are most susceptible, particularly when cold temperatures are accompanied by high winds.

Hypothermia occurs when the body fails to produce heat as fast as it loses it. Cold weather combined with hunger, fatigue, and dampness create a recipe for disaster. Symptoms are not always apparent to the victim. The early signs are numbness, shivering, slurring of words, dizzy spells; in extreme cases, these can progress to violent behavior, unconsciousness, and even death. The best treatment is to get the patient out of the cold, replace wet clothing with dry, slowly give hot liquids and sugary foods, and place the victim in a sleeping bag. Prevention is a better strategy; dress for cold in layers, including a waterproof outer layer, and wear a warm wool cap or other headgear.

CRIME

The provinces of Atlantic Canada enjoy one of the country's lowest crime rates. Violent crimes are infrequent; the most common crime is petty theft. If you must leave valuable items in your car unattended, keep them out of sight, preferably locked in the vehicle's trunk. Women have few difficulties traveling alone throughout the region.

Remember that cities such as St. John's are international ports with seamy (albeit interesting) bars and taverns at or near the working area of the waterfront; keep your wits about you, especially late at night. Better yet, leave these night scenes to the sailors and others who frequent the areas.

Both possession and sale of illicit drugs are considered serious crimes and are punishable with jail time, severe fines, or both. Furthermore, Canadians consider drinking while driving equally serious; the penalty on the first conviction is jail, heavy fine, or both. A conviction here or in your home country can be grounds for exclusion from Canada.

Royal Canadian Mounted Police (RCMP)

Despite the romantic image of the staid red-jacketed officer on horseback, Mounties (as they are most often called) nowadays favor the squad car as their mount of choice and wear a less colorful uniform. They are as ubiquitous a symbol of the country as the maple leaf, and they are similar to the highway patrol or state police in the United States. They operate throughout all the country's provinces and territories (except Ontario and Québec), complementing the work of local police.

Information and Services

MONEY

Unless noted otherwise, **prices quoted in this book are in Canadian currency.** Canadian currency is based on dollars and cents, with 100 cents equal to one dollar. Canada's money is issued in notes ($5, $10, and $20 are the most common) and coins (1, 5, 10, and 25 cents, and $1 and $2). The 11-sided, gold-colored $1 coin is known as a "loonie" for the bird featured on it. The unique $2 coin ("toonie," for "two loonies") is silver with a gold-colored insert.

By using credit and debit cards you eliminate the necessity of thinking about the exchange rate—the transaction and rate of exchange on the day of the transaction will automatically be reflected in the bill from your bank or credit-card company. On the downside, you'll always get a better exchange rate when dealing directly with a bank. You should always carry some cash, as places like farmers' markets and some bed and breakfasts do not accept debit or credit cards.

Costs

The cost of living in Atlantic Canada is lower than elsewhere in the country. For you, the visitor, this will be most apparent when paying for accommodations and meals. By planning ahead, having a tent, or traveling in the shoulder seasons, it is possible to get by on around $120 per person per day or less. Gasoline is sold in liters (3.78 liters equals 1 U.S. gallon) and is generally $1.20-1.40 a liter for regular unleaded.

Tipping charges are not usually added to your bill. You are expected to add a tip of 15 percent to the total amount for waiters and waitresses, barbers and hairdressers, taxi drivers, and other such service providers. Bellhops, doormen, and porters generally receive $1 per item of baggage.

Harmonized Sales Tax (HST)

A 13 percent Harmonized Sales Tax is levied on most goods and services purchased within Newfoundland and Labrador. The HST includes the 5 percent goods and services tax (GST) applied across Canada. At 9 percent, the provincial sales tax on Prince Edward Island is 1 percent higher than the other three provinces, for a combined total of 14 percent HST.

COMMUNICATIONS AND MEDIA

Postal Services

Canada Post (www.canadapost.ca) issues postage stamps that must be used on all mail posted in Canada. Letters and postcards sent within Canada are $1, to the United States $1.20, to other foreign destinations $2.50. Prices increase with the weight of the mailing. You can buy stamps at post offices (closed weekends), some hotel lobbies, airports, many retail outlets, and some newsstands.

Telephone Services

The country code for Canada is 1, the same as the United States. The provincial area code for Newfoundland and Labrador is 709. This prefix must be dialed for all long-distance calls, even in-province calls. Toll-free numbers have the 800, 888, 877, or 866 prefix, and may be good for the province, Atlantic Canada, Canada, North America, or, in the case of major hotel chains and car rental companies, worldwide.

To make an international call from Canada, dial the prefix 011 before the country code or dial 0 for operator assistance.

Public phones accept 5-, 10-, and 25-cent coins; local calls are $0.35-0.50, and most long-distance calls cost at least $2.50 for the first minute. The least expensive way to make long-distance calls from a public phone is with a **phone card.** These are available from convenience stores, newsstands, and gas stations.

Internet Access

All major hotels and most B&Bs have wireless Internet access. You'll also find free wireless Internet in most airports and cafés.

Newspapers and Magazines

Atlantic Canada is too expansive and diverse to be well covered by one newspaper, but plenty of regional and big-city papers are available. The *Globe and Mail* and *National Post* are distributed throughout the Atlantic provinces.

Canada's best-selling and most respected newsmagazine is *Maclean's*. *L'Actualité* is the French counterpart. *Newsweek, Time,* and other big American publications are available at drugstores, bookstores, and corner groceries.

WEIGHTS AND MEASURES

Canada uses the metric system, with temperature measured in degrees Celsius; liquid measurements in liters; solid weights in kilograms and metric tons; land areas in hectares; and distances in kilometers, meters, and centimeters. This newfangled system hasn't completely taken hold everywhere, and many locals still think in terms of the imperial system; expect to hear a lobster described in pounds, local distances given in miles, and the temperature expressed in Fahrenheit degrees.

The electrical voltage is 120 volts. The standard electrical plug configuration is the same as that used in the United States: two flat blades, often with a round third pin for grounding.

Time Zones

Officially, all of Newfoundland and Labrador is on **Newfoundland Standard Time (NST),** 30 minutes ahead of Atlantic Standard Time, although in reality only the island of Newfoundland and the southeastern Labrador communities on the Strait of Belle Isle adhere to NST.

Atlantic Standard Time is one hour ahead of Eastern Standard Time and four hours ahead of Pacific Standard Time.

Resources

Suggested Reading

NATURAL HISTORY

Grescoe, Taras. *Bottomfeeder*. Toronto: HarperCollins, 2008. An insight into the fisheries industry made more readable by the author's firsthand accounts of visits to the world's most important fisheries, including Nova Scotia.

Scott, Peter J. *Edible Plants of Atlantic Canada*. Portugal Cove, Newfoundland: Boulder Publications, 2014. A detailed field guide to around 60 edible plants and berries present in the region. Includes details on finding each one as well as recipes.

HUMAN HISTORY

Andrieux, J. P. *St. Pierre and Miquelon: A Fragment of France in North America*. Ottawa: O.T C. Press, 1986. One of the most thorough books about France's overseas province, the small volume details sightseeing within a historical context and is illustrated with historical photographs.

Campbell, Gary. *The Road to Canada*. Fredericton, New Brunswick: Goose Lane Editions, 2005. Tells the story of how river transportation—specifically on the Saint John and St. Lawrence Rivers—opened up central Canada for settlement.

De Mont, John. *Citizens Irving: K. C. Irving and His Legacy, The Story of Canada's Wealthiest Family*. Toronto: Doubleday Canada, 1991. The Irving family is very private, and this unofficial biography is stuffed with well-documented unfavorable and favorable facts, legends and speculation.

Major, Kevin. *As Near to Heaven by Sea: A History of Newfoundland and Labrador*. Toronto: Penguin, 2002. Lively yet full of detail, this is an excellent introduction to Newfoundland and Labrador's long and colorful history.

Rompkey, Ronald. *Grenfell of Labrador: A Biography*. Toronto: University of Toronto Press, 1991. Sir Wilfred Grenfell, the physician-missionary whose work left an indelible imprint on the province's remote areas, has had several biographers, but none as meticulous and incisive as Rompkey.

Slumkoski, Corey. *Inventing Atlantic Canada: Regionalism and the Maritime Reaction to Newfoundland's Entry into Canadian Confederation*. Toronto: University of Toronto Press, 2011. This hefty hardcover book tells the story of Newfoundland's 1949 entry into the Canadian confederation and its effect on the three Maritime provinces.

Tuck, James A., and Robert Grenier. *Red Bay, Labrador: World Whaling Capital, A.D. 1550–1660*. St John's, Newfoundland: Atlantic Archaeology, 1989. Archaeological discoveries provide the grist for relating the early Basque whaling industry. Splendid color photographs and black-and-white graphics.

SPORTS, CULTURE, AND CRAFTS

Mowat, Claire. *The Outport People.* Toronto: Key Porter Books, 2005. The wife of famed Canadian writer Farley Mowat describes the couple's time living in a remote Newfoundland village in the form of a fictional memoir.

Proulx, E. Annie. *The Shipping News.* New York: Touchstone, 1994. Pulitzer Prize–winning story of a widowed journalist rebuilding his life on the Newfoundland coast.

Story, G. M., W. J. Kirwin, and J. D. A. Widdowson, eds. *Dictionary of Newfoundland English.* Toronto: University of Toronto Press, 1990. The Newfoundlanders use their own version of the King's English—from "Aaron's rod," a roseroot's local name, to "zosweet," a Beothuk word for the ptarmigan. This remarkably researched compilation translates words and adds historical, geographical, and cultural insights.

RECREATION GUIDES AND GUIDEBOOKS

Broadhurst, Katie and Alexandra Fortin. *Hikes of Western Newfoundland.* Portugal Cove, Newfoundland: Boulder Publications, 2014. Details 60 hiking trails from Port-aux-Basque in the south to the tip of the Northern Peninsula and as far east as Twillingate. A large section of the book is devoted to Gros Morne National Park.

Gadd, Ben. *The Canadian Hiker's and Backpacker's Handbook.* Vancouver: Whitecap Books, 2008. Authored by a renowned expert, this is the best book for reading up on your backcountry and hiking skills.

Gillis, Rannis, and Ken Aiken. *Motorcycle Journeys Through Atlantic Canada.* Conway Center, New Hampshire: Whitehorse Press, 2011. A travel guidebook for motorcycle enthusiasts, the book covers routes through all four provinces, including the Cabot Trail.

National Geographic. *Guide to the National Parks of Canada.* Washington DC: National Geographic Society, 2011. This full-color guide was published to celebrate the centenary of the Canadian national park system.

O'Flaherty, Patrick. *Come Near at Your Peril: A Visitor's Guide to the Island of Newfoundland.* St. John's, Newfoundland: Breakwater Books, 1994. Often hilarious and always insightful, the author meanders across the island, explains the sights as no one but a Newfoundlander sees them, and reveals travel's potential tangles and torments.

MAGAZINES, MAPS, AND ATLASES

Canadian Geographic. Ottawa: Royal Canadian Geographical Society (www.canadiangeographic.ca). Bimonthly publication pertaining to Canada's natural and human histories and resources.

Downhome. St. John's, Newfoundland. Monthly magazine of everything Newfoundland and Labrador, from family stores to hints on growing gardens in northern climes (www.downhomelife.com).

Explore. Toronto. Bimonthly publication of adventure travel throughout Canada (www.explore-mag.com).

Hamilton, William B. *Place Names of Atlantic Canada.* Toronto: University of Toronto, 1996. Includes definitions for thousands of place-names throughout the region. Divided by province and then sorted alphabetically.

MapArt. Driving maps for all of Canada, street atlas for major cities, and folded maps of Atlantic Canada (www.mapart.com).

Meacham's Illustrated Historical Atlas of the Province of Prince Edward Island, 1880. Charlottetown, Prince Edward Island:

P.E.I. Historical Foundation, 1989. A helpful guide to tracing family roots.

Nature Canada. Ottawa. Seasonal e-newsletter of Nature Canada (www.naturecanada.ca).

Saltscapes. Bedford, Nova Scotia. Classy life-style magazine for Canada's east coast. Seven issues annually (www.saltscapes.com).

Internet Resources

TRAVEL PLANNING

Canadian Tourism Commission
www.canada.travel
Official tourism website for all of Canada.

Newfoundland and Labrador Tourism
www.newfoundlandlabrador.com
The first place to go when planning your trip to the region's largest province. This site in-cludes a distance calculator, order forms for brochures, and detailed events calendars.

PARKS

**Department of Environment
and Conservation**
www.env.gov.nl.ca/parks
Newfoundland and Labrador is dotted with provincial parks and wilderness preserves, and this website details them all.

Parks Canada
www.pc.gc.ca
Official website of the agency that manages Canada's national parks and national historic sites. Information includes general informa-tion, operating hours, and fees.

Parks Canada Campground Reservation Service
www.pccamping.ca
Use this website to make reservations for campsites in national parks.

GOVERNMENT

Atlantic Canada Online
www.acol.ca
An alliance of the four provincial governments

to disseminate databases of information to the public.

Citizenship and Immigration Canada
www.cic.gc.ca
Check this government website for anything related to entry to Canada.

Environment Canada
www.weather.gc.ca
Seven-day forecasts from across Canada, including more than 200 locations across Atlantic Canada. Includes weather archives such as seasonal trends, hurricane history, and sea ice movement.

Government of Canada
www.gc.ca
The official website of the Canadian government.

ACCOMMODATIONS

Bed and Breakfast Online
www.bbcanada.com
Easy-to-use tools for finding and reserving B&Bs that suit your budget and interests.

Hostelling International–Canada
www.hihostels.ca
Canadian arm of the worldwide organization.

TRANSPORTATION

Air Canada
www.aircanada.ca
Canada's national airline.

Marine Atlantic
www.marine-atlantic.ca
Use this website to make advance reservations for ferry travel between Nova Scotia and Newfoundland.

WestJet
www.westjet.com
Before booking with Air Canada, check out this airline for flights into Atlantic Canada from points west.

CONSERVATION

Atlantic Canada Conservation Data Centre
www.accdc.com
Some good information on what species you're likely to see and where, but mostly composed of charts and databases.

Canadian Parks and Wilderness Society
www.cpaws.org
A national nonprofit organization that is instrumental in highlighting conservation issues throughout Canada.

Ducks Unlimited Canada
www.ducks.ca
Respected wetlands protection organization represented by chapters in each of the four Atlantic Canada provinces.

Sierra Club Atlantic
http://atlantic.sierraclub.ca
Dedicated to preserving wilderness throughout the region. Currently active in fighting oil and gas development in the Gulf of St. Lawrence.

Starving Ocean
www.fisherycrisis.com
Filled with Canadian content, this private website contains articles related to seals, humpback whales, and the decline in cod stocks.

PUBLISHERS

Breakwater Books
www.breakwaterbooks.com
A Newfoundland and Labrador publishing house that specializes producing works by local authors.

Creative Book Publishing
www.creativebookpublishing.ca
This St. John's book publisher has expanded from its stable of local titles to include a catalog of over 200 books, many related to life in Newfoundland and Labrador.

Goose Lane Editions
www.gooselane.com
While all the best books on Atlantic Canada are detailed under *Suggested Reading,* check the website of this prolific Fredericton-based publisher for contemporary titles about the region.

Index

A

accommodations: 127-129
air travel: 122-123
Aleksandrs International Gallery of Fine Art: 52
Anglican Cathedral of St. John the Baptist: 18
animals: 106-110
Arches Provincial Park: 75
Argentia: 40
Arts and Culture Centre: 25
auto travel: 122, 123-124
Avalon Peninsula: 8, 35-41

B

Baccalieu Trail: 35-37
Bakeapple Folk Festival: 89
Barachois Pond Provincial Park: 64
Basilica Cathedral Museum: 18
Battle Harbour: 9, 92-93
beaches: Central and Western Newfoundland
    64-65, 69; Labrador 93
beer/breweries: 25, 29
Bell Island: 23
Beothuk Interpretation Site: 55, 60
bicycling: 24, 126
Bird Cove: 75-77
birds/bird-watching: general discussion 110;
    Central and Western Newfoundland 62;
    Labrador 93; St. John's and the Avalon
    Peninsula 22, 36, 37, 41
Blow Me Down Provincial Park: 62
Blue Hill Pond: 53
Boat Harbour: 46
Bonavista: 52
Bonavista Peninsula: 49-52
botanical gardens/arboretums: Central and
    Western Newfoundland 68; St. John's and
    the Avalon Peninsula 23
Bowring Park: 21
Boyd's Cove: 55-56
Brigus: 35
Broom Point: 68, 70
Burin: 46
Burin Peninsula: 46-48
Burnt Cape Ecological Reserve: 82
Butter Pot Provincial Park: 24

C

Cabot Tower: 20
camping: general discussion 129; Central and
    Western Newfoundland 54, 59, 62, 63, 64, 65,
    73-74, 81, 82; Labrador 98, 101; St. John's and
    the Avalon Peninsula 32-33, 38
Cape Anguille: 65
Cape Bonavista: 52
Cape Bonavista Lighthouse: 52
Cape Shore: 39-41
Cape Spear National Historic Site: 21-22
Cape St. Mary's Ecological Reserve: 8, 41
Captain Cook's Monument: 60
car travel: 122, 123-124
Cartwright: 93
Castle Hill National Historic Site: 40
Central and Western Newfoundland: 42-82;
    map 45
children, traveling with: 130-131
churches/temples: Central and Western
    Newfoundland 68; St. John's and the Avalon
    Peninsula 18, 19
Churchill Falls: 96-97
Clarenville: 49
climate: 103-104
Codroy Valley Provincial Park: 64-65
Colony of Avalon: 8, 38
Commissariat House: 19
Conception Bay Museum: 36
Cooperage, The: 50
Corner Brook: 60-64; map 61
Corner Brook Museum: 60
costs: 133
Cow Head: 68
crime: 132
Cuckold's Cove Trail: 20
Cupids: 36

DE

Daniel's Harbour: 75
Deep Cove Wintering Interpretation Site: 78
Deer Lake: 59-60
demographics: 118-119
Dildo: 37
disabilities, travelers with: 130
Discovery Centre: 69
Dock House Museum: 79
Dog Peninsula: 77
economy: 117-118
electricity: 134
Elephant Shop: 52
emergencies: Corner Brook 64; North West River
    96; St. John's 33
employment: 130

environmental issues: 104-105
expenses: 133

F
fauna: 106-110
Ferryland: 8, 38-39
ferry travel: 123
Festival 500 Growing the Voices: 26
Festival of Folk Song and Dance: 46
fish/fishing: 59, 69, 124-126
Fishing Point Park: 78
Flagstaff Hill Monument: 93
flora: 105-106
Flowers Cove: 8, 78
Fluvarium: 22-23
Forteau: 89

G
Gander: 54-55; map 55
Gannet Islands Ecological Reserve: 93
Gateway to Labrador Visitor Centre: 88
geography: 103-104
George C. Harris House: 47
George Street: 8, 26
George Street Festival: 26
golf: 22
government: 116-117
Government House: 19
Grand Bank: 47
Grand Falls-Windsor: 57-58
Grates Cove: 36
gratuities: 133
Green Family Forge: 50
Green Gardens: 70
Grenfell Handicrafts: 79
Grenfell House Museum: 79
Grenfell Interpretation Centre: 78
Grenfell, Wilfred: 90
Gros Morne Mountain: 70
Gros Morne National Park: 8, 66-74; map 67
Gros Morne Theatre Festival: 71

H
Happy Valley-Goose Bay: 94-96; map 95
Harbour Grace: 36
Hawthorne Cottage National Historic Site: 35
health: 131-132
Heart's Content: 36-37
Hebron Mission National Historic Site: 100
Heritage Trail (Terra Nova): 53
Heritage Walk: 47
hiking: general discussion 124; Central and
    Western Newfoundland 53, 70; St. John's and
    the Avalon Peninsula 20, 22, 23, 24, 39
Hiscock House: 50

history: 110-116
Hopedale: 99

IJK
icebergs: 56-57, 58, 79
insurance: 131
Internet access: 134
Irish Loop: 39
itineraries: 8-9
James J. O'Mara Pharmacy Museum: 18-19
Jersey Rooms: 88
Johnson Geo Centre: 19-20
Jordi Bonet Murals: 79
kayaking/canoeing: Central and Western
    Newfoundland 53; Labrador 93

L
Labrador: 83-101; maps 86
Labrador City: 98
Labrador Heritage Museum: 95
Labrador Institute: 95
Labrador Interpretation Centre: 95
Labrador Inuit Association: 97
Labrador, map of: 3
Labrador Straits: 88-93
La Manche Provincial Park: 37-38
Lance Cove: 24
language: 120
L'Anse Amour: 9, 89-91
L'Anse-au-Clair: 88-89
L'Anse aux Meadows: 9, 80-82
L'Anse aux Meadows National Historic Site: 9, 80
Lark Harbour: 62
Lester Garland House: 50
Lighthouse Picnics: 8, 38
lighthouses: Central and Western Newfoundland
    52, 57, 65, 68; Labrador 90; St. John's and the
    Avalon Peninsula 21-22
Lobster Cove Head: 68, 70
Long Point: 57

M
magazines: 134
mail: 133
Makkovik: 98-99
Makkovik Craft Centre: 99
Mallard Cottage: 8, 30
Marble Mountain: 9, 62
Mariners' Memorial: 47
Maritime Archaic Burial Mound National Historic
    Site: 89
Mary March Provincial Museum: 57, 60
Mary's Harbour: 91-92
measurements: 134
Memorial University Botanical Garden: 23

Mercantile Premises: 50
Mile One Centre: 26
Miquelon: 47-48
Mistaken Point Ecological Reserve: 39
Mockbeggar Plantation: 52
money: 133
Moore's Handicrafts: 88
Museum of Whales and Things: 76

N

Nain: 99-101
national parks: general discussion 124, 125;
    Gros Morne 66-74; Terra Nova 53-54; Torngat
    Mountains 100-101
Native Peoples: 119-120
Newfoundland Insectarium: 59
Newfoundland, map of: 2
Newfoundland Symphony Orchestra: 26
Newman Wine Vaults: 19
newspapers: 134
Norseman Restaurant: 81
Norstead: 81
North Atlantic Aviation Museum: 54
Northern Lights Military Museum: 94
North Head Trail: 20
North Sydney: 34, 40, 66
North West River: 95-96

OP

Outport Trail: 53
packing tips: 131
parks and gardens: 21
Petite Miquelon: 47
phones: 133-134
Pippy Park: 22-23, 24
Pisolet Bay Provincial Park: 82
Placentia: 40-41
plane travel: 122-123
Plantation Site: 36
plants: 105-106
Plum Point: 76-77
Point Amour Lighthouse: 90
politics: 116-117
Port au Choix National Historic Site: 8, 75-76
Port-aux-Basques: 65-66
Port Union: 51
postal services: 133
prescriptions: 131
provincial parks: general discussion 124; Central
    and Western Newfoundland 59, 62, 64-65,
    75, 82; St. John's and the Avalon Peninsula 24,
    37-38
Provincial Seamen's Museum: 47

QR

Quidi Vidi: 8, 20-21
Quidi Vidi Battery: 21
Quidi Vidi Lake: 20
Quidi Vidi Village: 20
Railway Coastal Museum: 19
Raleigh: 82
Red Bay: 9, 91
religion: 120
rental cars: 124
Resource Centre for the Arts: 25
resources: 135-138
Rocky Harbour: 8, 68
Rooms, The: 8, 16, 18
Royal Canadian Mounted Police (RCMP): 132
Royal St. John' Regatta: 25
Ryan Premises: 52

S

safety: 131-132
Salmonid Interpretation Centre: 57
Salmonier Nature Park: 39
Sandy Pond: 53
scenic drive: 62
scuba diving/snorkeling:24
Shakespeare by the Sea Festival: 26
Shamrock Festival: 33
shopping: 127
Signal Hill: 19-20
Signal Hill National Historic Site: 8, 20
Signal Hill Tattoo: 26
Silent Witness Memorial:55
Sir Richard Squires Provincial Park: 59
spectator sports: 26, 127
Squire Cove: 88
St. Anthony: 78-80
St. Barbe: 77
Steady Brook Falls: 62
Stephenville: 64
St. John's: 8, 10-34; maps 14, 17
St. John's and the Avalon Peninsula: 10-41;
    map 13
St. Mary's Church: 68
St.-Pierre: 47-48
St. Thomas's Anglican Church: 19
study opportunities: 130
Summer in the Bight: 50-51
swimming: 53, 64

T

Tablelands: 8, 69, 70
taxes: 133
telephones: 133-134
Terra Nova National Park: 53-54
Thorndyke House: 47

INDEX

thrombolites: 8, 78
time zones: 134
tipping: 133
Torngat Mountains National Park: 100-101
transportation: 122-124
Trapper's Brook Animal Display: 95
Trinity: 8, 49-51
Trinity Society Museum: 50
Trinity Visitor Centre: 50
Trout River: 69
Twillingate: 56-57
Twillingate Museum: 56

UVWXYZ

Voisey's Bay: 100
voltage: 134
Wabana: 23
Wabush: 98

waterfalls: 57, 62
water sports: 126-127
weather: 103-104
weights and measures: 134
Western Brook Pond: 8, 45, 70, 71
Wetland Interpretation Centre: 64
whale-watching: 37
White Elephant Museum: 99
wildlife/wildlife-watching: general discussion
    106-110; Central and Western Newfoundland
    53; St. John's and the Avalon Peninsula 22,
    37, 39
wine/wineries: 19
Winterhouse: 64
winter sports: 62, 127
winter travel: 132
Witless Bay Ecological Reserve: 8, 37
Wunderstrands: 93
YellowBelly Brewery: 25, 29

List of Maps

Front Map
Newfoundland: 2
Labrador: 3

St. John's and the Avalon Peninsula
St. John's and the Avalon Peninsula: 13
St. John's : 14
Downtown St. John's: 17

Central and Western Newfoundland
Central and Western Newfoundland: 45
Gander: 55
Corner Brook: 61
Gros Morne National Park 67

Labrador
Labrador: 85
Happy Valley-Goose Bay: 95

Photo Credits

Also Available

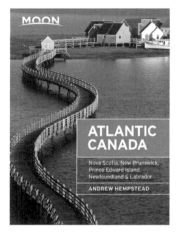

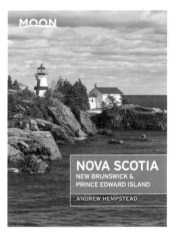

MAP SYMBOLS

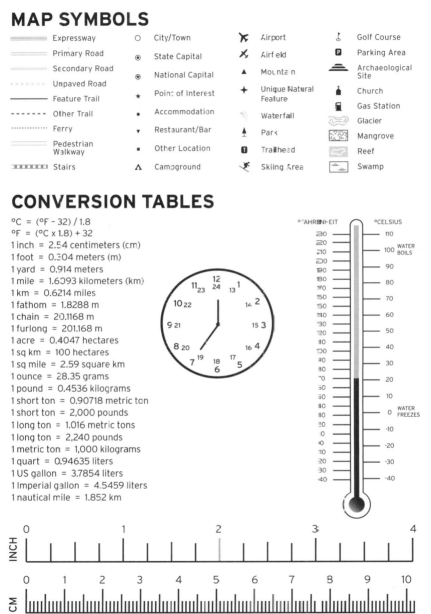

≋ Expressway	○ City/Town	✈ Airport	⌟ Golf Course
Primary Road	◉ State Capital	✘ Airfield	🅿 Parking Area
Secondary Road	◉ National Capital	▲ Mountain	≜ Archaeological Site
Unpaved Road	★ Point of Interest	✛ Unique Natural Feature	🛉 Church
Feature Trail	● Accommodation		Gas Station
Other Trail	▼ Restaurant/Bar	Waterfall	Glacier
Ferry	■ Other Location	▲ Park	Mangrove
Pedestrian Walkway	▲ Campground	▯ Trailhead	Reef
Stairs		⛷ Skiing Area	Swamp

CONVERSION TABLES

°C = (°F - 32) / 1.8
°F = (°C x 1.8) + 32
1 inch = 2.54 centimeters (cm)
1 foot = 0.304 meters (m)
1 yard = 0.914 meters
1 mile = 1.6093 kilometers (km)
1 km = 0.6214 miles
1 fathom = 1.8288 m
1 chain = 20.1168 m
1 furlong = 201.168 m
1 acre = 0.4047 hectares
1 sq km = 100 hectares
1 sq mile = 2.59 square km
1 ounce = 28.35 grams
1 pound = 0.4536 kilograms
1 short ton = 0.90718 metric ton
1 short ton = 2,000 pounds
1 long ton = 1.016 metric tons
1 long ton = 2,240 pounds
1 metric ton = 1,000 kilograms
1 quart = 0.94635 liters
1 US gallon = 3.7854 liters
1 Imperial gallon = 4.5459 liters
1 nautical mile = 1.852 km

MOON NEWFOUNDLAND & LABRADOR
Avalon Travel
An imprint of Perseus Books
A Hachette Book Group company
1700 Fourth Street
Berkeley, CA 94710, USA
www.moon.com

Editor: Kimberly Ehart
Series Manager: Kathryn Ettinger
Copy Editor: Ann Siefert
Production Designer: Sarah Wildfang
Cover Design: Faceout Studios, Charles Brock
Interior Design: Domini Dragoone
Moon Logo: Tim McGrath
Map Editor: Albert Angulo
Cartographers: Austin Ehrhardt and Brian Shotwell
Proofreader: Rachael Sablik
Indexer: Greg Jewett

ISBN-13: 978-1-63121-570-4

Printing History
1st Edition — July 2017
5 4 3 2 1

Text © 2017 by Andrew Hempstead.
Maps © 2017 by Avalon Travel.
All rights reserved.

Some photos and illustrations are used by permission and are the property of the original copyright owners.

Front cover photo: Michael Runkel | Getty Images
Back cover photo: Andrew Hempstead

Printed in Canada by Friesens